THE NORMAN WAIT HARRIS
MEMORIAL FOUNDATION

THE Harris Foundation Lectures at the University of Chicago have been made possible through the generosity of the heirs of Norman Wait Harris and Emma Gale Harris, who donated to the University a fund to be known as "The Norman Wait Harris Memorial Foundation" on January 27, 1923. The letter of gift contains the following statement:

It is apparent that a knowledge of world-affairs was never of more importance to Americans than today. The spirit of distrust which pervades the Old World is not without its effect upon our own country. How to combat this disintegrating tendency is a problem worthy of the most serious thought. Perhaps one of the best methods is the promotion of a better understanding of other nations through wisely directed educational effort.

The purpose of the foundation shall be the promotion of a better understanding on the part of American citizens of the other peoples of the world, thus establishing a basis for improved international relations and a more enlightened world-order. The aim shall always be to give accurate information, not to propagate opinion.

Annual Institutes have been held at the University of Chicago since the summer of 1924. This series of volumes includes the lectures there delivered, in essentially their original form.

THE CRISIS OF DEMOCRACY

THE UNIVERSITY OF CHICAGO PRESS
CHICAGO, ILLINOIS

—

THE BAKER & TAYLOR COMPANY
NEW YORK

THE CAMBRIDGE UNIVERSITY PRESS
LONDON

THE MARUZEN-KABUSHIKI-KAISHA
TOKYO, OSAKA, KYOTO, FUKUOKA, SENDAI

THE COMMERCIAL PRESS, LIMITED
SHANGHAI

THE CRISIS
OF DEMOCRACY

[LECTURES ON THE HARRIS FOUNDATION 1938]

BY

WILLIAM E. RAPPARD

Professor at the University of Geneva
Director of the Graduate Institute
of International Studies, Geneva

THE UNIVERSITY OF CHICAGO PRESS
CHICAGO · ILLINOIS

COMPOSED AND PRINTED BY THE UNIVERSITY OF CHICAGO PRESS
CHICAGO, ILLINOIS, U.S.A.

FOREWORD

The lectures here reproduced were delivered at the Fourteenth Institute under the Norman Wait Harris Memorial Foundation held at the University of Chicago from August 2 to August 18, 1938. The Institute was devoted to "The Crisis of Democracy," and the public lectures were given by William E. Rappard, of Geneva, Switzerland. He is professor of economics at the University of Geneva, director of the Graduate Institute of International Studies at Geneva, and a member of the Permanent Mandates Commission of the League of Nations. He has frequently represented Switzerland in the League of Nations Assembly and is the author of numerous books and articles on political, economic, and international problems, including *International Relations as Viewed from Geneva* (1925), *Uniting Europe* (1930), *The Geneva Experiment* (1931), and *The Government of Switzerland* (1936). He edited and contributed to the volume entitled *The World Crisis* by professors of the Graduate Institute of International Studies, published in 1938.

Because of his practical experience in the workings of democratic institutions in Switzerland, his intimate association with efforts to organize world-

FOREWORD

politics democratically, and his studies of the history and theory of democracy, Professor Rappard was the first choice of the committee in charge of the Harris Institute to lecture on this subject. His lectures, which were received enthusiastically, disclose the inherent difficulties of democracy and the circumstances which have challenged it in many countries since the World War. Professor Rappard, however, does not despair of modern democracy, but rather questions the solidity and the longevity of modern dictatorships.

In addition to the lectures by Professor Rappard, discussion conferences were organized at the Harris Institute, at which members of the staff, graduate students at the University summer session, and visitors to the Institute were provided an opportunity to discuss particular phases of the problem.

The program of the Institute follows:

PUBLIC LECTURES BY W. E. RAPPARD

(Leon Mandel Hall)

I. Tuesday, August 2, 8:30 P.M.—Introductory: "Democracy and Its Crisis"
II. Thursday, August 4, 4:30 P.M.—"The Rise of Democracy in Europe"
III. Tuesday, August 9, 4:30 P.M.—"The World War and the Fate of Democracy"
IV. Thursday, August 11, 4:30 P.M.—"The Rise of Post-war Dictatorships, Communist and Fascist"

FOREWORD

V. Tuesday, August 16, 4:30 P.M.—"The Evolution of Democracy in Surviving Democracies"
VI. Thursday, August 18, 4:30 P.M.—"The Future of Democracy"

DISCUSSION CONFERENCES

(Burton Court)

I. Thursday, August 4, 7:30 P.M.—HARLEY F. MACNAIR,
Leader: "Democracy and the Far East"
II. Tuesday, August 9, 7:30 P.M.—MALBONE W. GRAHAM,
Leader: "Democracy and Eastern Europe"
III. Thursday, August 11, 7:30 P.M.—WILLIAM E. RAPPARD,
Leader: "Democracy and Central Europe"
IV. Tuesday, August 16, 7:30 P.M.—WILLIAM E. RAPPARD,
Leader: "Democracy and Western Europe"
V. Thursday, August 18, 7:30 P.M.—ROBERT REDFIELD,
Leader: "Democracy and the Americas"

QUINCY WRIGHT

UNIVERSITY OF CHICAGO
August 1938

TABLE OF CONTENTS

〖 xi 〗

TABLE OF CONTENTS

〖 xii 〗

TABLE OF CONTENTS

CHAPTER I

INTRODUCTORY

Of all the startling features of the tragically unexpected, but intensely interesting, age in which we
are living, the political phenomenon we are to examine in this study is perhaps the most unforeseen.
The phenomenon so aptly defined by the Greek
formula of "the crisis of democracy" has indeed
taken civilized mankind completely unawares.

For the generation which awoke to conscious
citizenship toward the beginnings of the present
century, no general fact seemed better established
than the reign of democracy in the modern world.
Of this reign the preceding generations had witnessed the gradual advent with mingled feelings,
but with the growing conviction of the inevitable.
Furthermore, the triumph of democracy seemed as
easy to explain as impossible to avoid. Knowledge
and reason appeared readily to indorse the intui-
tions of instinct.

Had not the industrial revolution overthrown
feudalism throughout western Europe and correspondingly enhanced the position of the bourgeoisie
which it had enriched? What principle of authority
could be substituted for that of birth, upon which
feudalism had rested for centuries, if it were not

selection by the many of the ablest and the most popular? Had not the example of the political developments in Great Britain and of the revolt of the American colonies, as well as the teachings of the French philosophers and the contagion of the French Revolution, all tended to plow up the soil of traditional society? Had they not all tended also to sow thereon the seeds which under the warm sun of improving public education could not but sooner or later produce a harvest of democracy? And were not democratic institutions spreading from the countries most advanced in economic and political development, where by the middle of the nineteenth century they were already well rooted, to those states whose evolution, even if retarded, was clearly proceeding in the same direction?

Thus Sir Henry Sumner Maine could write in 1885: "Democracy is commonly described as having an inherent superiority over every other form of government. It is supposed to advance with an irresistible and preordained movement."[1]

Thus also Lecky, whose well-known misgivings effectively protected him against any suspicion of wishful thinking, declared in 1896: "I do not think that anyone who seriously considers the force and universality of the movement of our generation in the direction of democracy can doubt that this conception of government will necessarily, at least for

[1] *Popular Government* (London, 1885), p. viii.

INTRODUCTORY

a considerable time, dominate in all civilized countries."[2]

The World War in no way shook, but on the contrary re-enforced, the universal confidence in the
inevitability of the ultimate triumph of popular
government. Had it not been waged in order to
make the world safe for democracy, and had it not
been won by the democratic allied and associated
states? Was their victory not due to the democratic spirit of their peoples? Had not this spirit,
while maintaining their own morale by its example, shattered that of their enemies, still subjected to the antiquated rule of absolute monarchy? And did not the return of peace coincide
with the establishment all over Europe of democratic institutions set up on the ruins of the col-
lapsed thrones of kings and emperors?

As Lord Bryce wrote on the morrow of these
developments:

Within the hundred years that now lie behind us what
changes have passed upon the world! Nearly all the monarchies of the Old World have been turned into democracies.
The States of the American Union have grown from thirteen
to forty-eight. While twenty new republics have sprung up in
the Western hemisphere, five new democracies have been
developed out of colonies within the British dominions.
There are now more than one hundred representative assemblies at work all over the earth legislating for self-governing
communities; and the proceedings of nearly all of these are

[2] William Edward Hartpole Lecky, *Democracy and Liberty* (2 vols.;
London, 1896), I, 212.

recorded in the press. Thus the materials for a study of free governments have been and are accumulating so fast that the most diligent student cannot keep pace with the course of political evolution in more than a few out of these many countries.

A not less significant change has been the universal acceptance of democracy as the normal and natural form of government. Seventy years ago, as those who are now old can well remember, the approaching rise of the masses to power was regarded by the educated classes of Europe as a menace to order and prosperity. Then the word Democracy awakened dislike or fear. Now it is a word of praise. Popular power is welcomed, extolled, worshipped. The few whom it repels or alarms rarely avow their sentiments. Men have almost ceased to study its phenomena because these now seem to have become part of the established order of things. The old question,—What is the best form of government? is almost obsolete because the centre of interest has been shifting. It is not the nature of democracy, nor even the variety of the shapes it wears, that are to-day in debate, but rather the purposes to which it may be turned, the social and economic changes it may be used to effect; yet its universal acceptance is not a tribute to the smoothness of its working, for discontent is everywhere rife, while in some countries the revolutionary spirit is passing into forms heretofore undreamt of, one of which looms up as a terrifying spectre.[3]

When these words were first published in 1921, the tide had already begun to turn. Kerensky had, to be sure, triumphed over czarism in 1917. But hardly six months later Lenin had triumphed over Kerensky and conjured up the terrifying specter to which Lord Bryce referred. The Russian democratic revolution, which had been greeted as a flash

[3] James Bryce, *Modern Democracies* (2 vols.; 3d ed.; London, 1923), I, 4-5.

of political freedom, soon appeared comparable rather to a brief eclipse of the spirit of intolerance which had ever before and has ever since prevailed on the banks of the Volga. And shortly the march on Rome was to show that the much-heralded triumph of democracy was to be as short-lived, as precarious, and as partial, as it had seemed brilliant, definitive, and universal.

When democracy came to be challenged by some and soon denounced by many as the idol of a false and obsolete faith, President A. Lawrence Lowell, of Harvard, that penetrating student of political history, must have recalled with melancholy satisfaction an extraordinarily shrewd remark he had made on the eve of the World War. Toward the close of his *Public Opinion and Popular Government*, published in 1913, he had written:

> Many people feel that because popular government is new it must be lasting. They know it is a vital part of the spirit of the age, which they assume to be permanent. But that is the one thing the spirit of the age never is. It would not deserve its name if it were; and when any spirit of the age has become universally recognized, it is time to scan the horizon for signs of a new era.[4]

Since the publication of Lord Bryce's *Modern Democracies* in 1921, Europe and the world have witnessed the dramatic antidemocratic reaction which it is our purpose here to examine. Not only have most of the new liberal constitutions col-

[4] (New York, 1913), p. 303.

lapsed like the light huts of an American mining town, with whose mushroom growth their spread may be compared, but the cyclone of the authoritarian reaction which has passed over the world has even shaken the institutions of democracy where they were older. So that today, "popular power," of which Lord Bryce wrote fifteen years ago that it was "welcomed, extolled, worshipped," has come to be cursed in some quarters, apologetically defended in others, but questioned and indeed qualified everywhere.

Must we conclude therefrom that the triumph of modern democracy is to be as short-lived as it is recent? Is, in fact, the government of the people, by the people, and for the people to perish from the earth, in spite of the generous genius of the philosophers who conceived its ideals in the eighteenth century, of the wisdom of the statesmen who shaped its destinies in the nineteenth, and of the devotion of the millions who have already bled in its defense in the twentieth?

That is the momentous question which we are inevitably led to ask ourselves in the course of this study, a question on which the past may throw some light, but which an uncertain future alone can answer.

Let us make it quite clear from the outset of this discussion that, while we shall seek to interpret this past with complete impartiality, we, like our Swiss fellow-citizens generally, could not look upon a future destructive and exclusive of democracy with any feelings but those of humiliation and indeed of despair.

These preliminary remarks were intended solely to outline the general topic under discussion and to show both its scope and its exceptional interest. We have now to approach it more closely and, first of all, to gain a more intimate view of the true nature of democracy whose crisis we are to consider.

What do we mean by democracy? No term is easier glibly to define, but no form of government is more elusive. If under the shell of the word, which has been used in much the same sense for the last twenty-five centuries, we seek to discover the kernel of fact it covers, we immediately encounter almost insuperable difficulties. Indeed, as my illustrious fellow-citizen Rousseau wrote in 1762 in the work which probably did more than any one other to bring about the triumph of what is commonly called modern democracy: "If we take the term in its strictest sense, there never has existed nor ever will exist a true democracy. It is contrary to the nature of things that the many govern and the few be governed."[5]

[5] Jean-Jacques Rousseau, *Le Contrat social* (1762), Vol. III, chap. iv.

THE CRISIS OF DEMOCRACY

Ten years before, Rousseau's British contemporary, David Hume, had already remarked that "nothing appears more surprising to those who consider human affairs with a philosophical eye than the easiness with which the many are governed by the few."[6]

Today, in view of the frantic efforts made by the governing few, be they individual dictators or democratic politicians, to become and to remain popular with the governed many, no one is likely to be struck by the ease which so impressed David Hume. But no one will deny that in our times, hardly less than in his, the many are still in fact governed by the few. Shall we then dismiss the whole subject by declaring democracy as an institution to be an illusion and democracy as a term a mere misnomer?

Such, we may note, is the usual attitude of contemporary dictators. When attacking the form of government they most abhor, they are prone to divide their oratorical energies between the denunciation of its failings and the denial of its existence. This position, while obviously self-contradictory, is none the less, and, in fact, all the more, enlightening. It shows that however we define democracy, it is a regime inherently and essen-

---

[6] David Hume, "Of the First Principles of Government," *Essays Literary, Moral and Political*, No. IV; cited by Arthur N. Holcombe, *The Foundations of the Modern Commonwealth* (New York, 1923), p. 1.

tially opposed to that of contemporary dictator-ships and therefore, if nothing else, a historical reality. Like all historical realities it must be susceptible, if not of nice logical definition, at least of faithful description.

That democracy is not and cannot simply be regarded as the rule of the people, that is, of all the people, is obvious for many reasons.

First, if it were synonymous with the rule of all the people, the people would always have to be unanimous, because if they were not the dissenting minorities would be ruled and not ruling. Now no people, however united on fundamental issues, have ever been known to be unanimous, that is, without dissenting minorities subject to a will contrary to their own.

Second, if democracy were synonymous with the rule of the majority, the majority would always have to be endowed not only with the rights of active citizenship but also with the faculty and with the will to exercise these rights, which they seldom if ever are. We may note that important bodies of the population may be deprived of such rights even under the most popular forms of government by reason of their sex, as in my country for instance; of their nationality, as almost everywhere; or of their age, as everywhere. But far more important and more significant still, the majority of the male, national, and adult citizens themselves, even in the most enlightened states, are never truly free and able to exercise an equal share of influence on the shaping of public policies. Many circumstances, from the most natural and therefore least evitable—such as poor health and inferior intelligence—to those which may be held to be artificial and therefore temporary—such as poverty and ignorance—everywhere prevent the regime commonly known as democracy from being defined as that in which the majority of the people truly rule.

Finally, it must be stressed that the business of government is, for technical reasons, necessarily reserved for the few, whom the many may more or less freely choose and more or less effectively control, but from whose station of power and influence the many can never oust them, except to make room for other equally small minorities. What Rousseau and Hume had already observed in their day is not less true in our own. The many, to be sure, have become better educated, and the institutions and techniques of government have been developed so as to allow them more generally, more readily, and more freely to express their will. But these conditions, favorable for the establishment and working of democracy, have been more than compensated by the difficulties resulting from the increase in numbers of the population and especially by the enlarged functions of the state and the correspondingly enhanced complexity of the machinery of government.

For all these reasons, which it would be easy but unnecessary and wearisome to elaborate still further, democracy can no more today than a century and a half ago, when it existed only in the dreams of certain philosophers, be regarded and defined simply as the rule of the people or even of the majority of the people.

Still we all feel both that democracy must and that it can be distinguished from other forms of government. It must be, not only for the purposes of this study, but because, especially in our age of challenged and fluctuating values, it is essential that we know and understand what it is exactly in our political heritage that we cherish and may be called upon to defend against its enemies. And as it must be, so it can be. Are we not all more or less conscious of the characteristic features of this heritage even if we are at a loss to devise a clear and concise formula which would do them full justice?

This embarrassment is not in itself at all surprising. It is due simply to the extreme complexity and biological nature of the object under discussion. If democracy as we understand it were a strictly juristic concept, it would be as easy to define as is a perfect geometrical circle. It is, however, not a logical notion but a piece of social reality. Its definition therefore presents the same difficulties as would the complete and faithful description of all that is contained within a circle of say a mile in diameter, drawn in an area inhabited by a half-urban and half-rural heterogeneous human community.

In describing such a community the careful and clear-sighted analyst would emphasize its characteristic features so as to reveal its individuality and to distinguish it from all its neighbors. Still, he would doubtless find it impossible to make any general statement about it that would be absolutely true of all its members. If, for instance, he were led by his observations and comparisons to declare it to be prosperous, healthy, and law abiding, he would not thereby imply that it was without its paupers, its invalids, and its criminals.

As with the description of any human community, so with that of democracy. To define it etymologically is, as we have seen, to evoke an abstract, unreal, and unrealizable ideal. In order to pry into and to picture its real nature, it is necessary to discover and to stress certain of its distinctive traits, even if thereby full justice be not done to all the minor characteristics of all historical democracies.

These distinctive traits will stand out most clearly, we believe, if we consider the historical origins of modern democracy. While postponing a closer examination of these origins until our next chapter, we may note that all popular movements tending toward what is commonly called democracy in Great Britain, on the continent of Europe, as well as in America, presented a dual character. On the one hand, they were protests and revolts against special privilege. On the other, they were protests and revolts against political restraint. Whether arising out of particular grievances due to material suffering or to injured pride, or whether inspired by abstract principles of natural justice, or whether, as has more generally been the case, such grievances and such principles have both been simultaneously invoked, modern democratic revolutions have always chosen for their watchwords "liberty and equality."

Thus when the authors of the American Declaration of Independence declared that governments derived "their just powers from the consent of the governed," they laid down what may be held to be the principle of democracy. But in their view this principle was itself based on something still more fundamental; namely, on certain truths declared to be self-evident. What were these truths?

First, that "all men were created equal." And second, that these equal creatures were "endowed with certain inalienable rights," among which were "life, liberty and the pursuit of happiness." The justification of government, that is, of a social organization armed with coercive powers, thus resided in the necessity of protecting the equality and the liberty of man. The form of government best calculated to assure this protection was that deriving its authority from the consent of the governed.

What was primary in the eyes of the founders of the American independence were the individual rights of equality and liberty. Democracy, however important, was but secondary—a necessary means toward an absolute end. As such it was at its inception clearly subordinated to its purpose, which dominated its spirit and permeated its structure.

It is not for me to explain to an American audience how and why this political philosophy inspired by the British and French liberals of the seventeenth and eighteenth centuries exactly suited the temper and the needs of the men of 1776. Injured in their economic interests as well as in their personal pride and sense of dignity by the policies of a government over which they had no control, and no longer content humbly to petition for redress, they boldly challenged the authority of that government itself. They did so in the name of liberty and equality, abstract rights which they declared to be inalienable by nature. Thus was American democracy born of the goddess of natural justice, impregnated by the protests of materially and morally discontented British colonists.

INTRODUCTORY

The birth of French democracy in the course of the same generation took place under very similar circumstances and for very similar reasons.

On the banks of the Seine, as along the coast of North America, discontent was rife. The mass of the population complained of excessive and unequal taxation and their intellectual leaders of unjustified restrictions on their individual liberty. Unable to secure redress from their traditional masters, they revolted against them in the name of those natural rights of liberty and equality which they were denied by the laws of the land.

In order that these laws should be altered, the supreme legislative power was to pass from the king to the nation. Popular government was set up, not so much by reason of any inherent virtues of its own, as because it was deemed necessary to establish and to safeguard the fundamental rights of the individual. In order to show it, let us but quote from the beginning of the first *déclaration des droits de l'homme et du citoyen* adopted by the French revolutionary authorities as early as October 2, 1789. The preamble and the first articles of this declaration read as follows:

Preamble.—The representatives of the French people constituting the National Assembly, convinced that the public misfortunes and the corruption of governments are due solely to ignorance and to the fact that the rights of man have been forgotten or trodden under foot, have decided in a solemn declaration to proclaim the natural, inalienable and sacred rights of man, in order that this declaration, being constantly before the minds of all members of the social body, may ever recall to them their rights and their duties; in order that the decisions of the legislative and executive authorities, being at all moments considered in the light of the purpose of the institution of government, may be more respected; in order that the complaints of the citizens, being from now on based on simple and indisputable principles, may ever contribute to the maintenance of the Constitution and to the happiness of all.

In consequence whereof the National Assembly recognizes and declares, in the presence and under the auspices of the Supreme Being, the following to be the rights of man and citizen:

I. All men are born and remain free and equal in rights; social distinctions are to be founded on public utility only.

II. The end of every political society is the preservation of the natural and inalienable rights of man. These rights are liberty, property, security and resistance to oppression.

III. The principle of all sovereignty resides essentially in the nation. No body, no individual, shall exert any authority which is not expressly derived from it.

As these statements clearly show, in France as in America at the close of the eighteenth century, liberty and equality of the individual were the idols and democracy the temple in which these idols were to be enshrined.

In Great Britain, the third of the three great contemporary democracies, the historical evolution was essentially different, although its final goal was not dissimilar.

The evolution was essentially different, first, in that it was far more gradual and less spectacular, and second, in that the erection of the two idols in the temple of democracy was not simultaneous, as in America and in France. As Macaulay wrote in 1848 in the first chapter of his *History of England*:

> The present constitution of our country is, to the constitution under which she flourished five hundred years ago, what the tree is to the sapling, what the man is to the boy. The alteration has been great. Yet there never was a moment at which the chief part of what existed was not old.[7]

The "chief part" of the unwritten constitution of Great Britain has always been its defense of liberty. Ever since the days of the Magna Charta in the early thirteenth century and even before, throughout all the storms of the seventeenth with its Petition of Right in 1628 and its Declaration of Right in 1689, and until the present day, it has been the proud boast of every Englishman that his country has been the citadel of human freedom. Although that liberty, guaranteed alike to all, was not without its inherent affinities to equality, the egalitarian ideal as such has never had the same hold on the British as on the French people. Although equality before the law has been a fundamental principle in Great Britain as in all other civilized states, political equality, as exemplified by universal suffrage, has been only recently achieved there.

[7] Thomas Babington Macaulay, *The History of England from the Accession of James the Second* (Fireside ed.; Boston and New York, 1910), I, 25.

And even today the prestige and indeed the popular favor still enjoyed by such institutions as the Crown, the Court, and the House of Lords, show that complete equality, as understood in the United States and on the continent of Europe, is not one of the fundamental tenets of British political philosophy.

Privileges seem revolting to the average Englishman only when they are abused, as was recently shown by certain royal incidents, matrimonial and prematrimonial. When, as in the distribution of honors or in the creation of new peers, privileges appear to be the reward of exceptional merit, they seem to give rise to more sympathetic and sometimes amused satisfaction than to hostile criticism. The British democrat may well subscribe to the American declaration that "all men were created equal," and even to its French revolutionary counterpart that "all men are born and remain free and equal in rights," but he is inclined to stress the qualifying clause of the latter statement to the effect that "social distinctions are to be founded on public utility only."

In spite of his less rhetorical insistence on abstract equality, it would be folly to deny the Englishman's devotion to democracy. No less than his American and perhaps even more than his French cousin is he determined to see the affairs of his country conducted in accordance with the will of the people and the individual rights of each subject assured of an equal measure of public respect.

And that to us is the essence of democracy.[8]

Thus understood—and we believe it is generally so understood today—democracy is undergoing a crisis. What do we mean by this statement and what is our justification for making it?

By the crisis of democracy we mean the change which has come over men's minds in all countries since the World War with respect to the institutions and indeed to the ideals of popular government. Our justification for asserting the existence of this change we find in two distinct spheres.

On the one hand, we see that many countries have done away with what democratic institutions they possessed, and we hear their leading statesmen expressly and often violently repudiating the ideals of democracy. Moreover, still more significant even if less dramatic, we see, on the other hand, that also in those other countries which remain true to the fundamentals of democracy, these fundamentals are being challenged by vociferous minorities and questioned, or at least thoughtfully reconsidered, by most unprejudiced observers.

The facts regarding the recent establishment of antidemocratic dictatorships on the ruins of demo-

[8] Cf. M. Bourquin, "The Crisis of Democracy," in *The World Crisis* (London, 1938), p. 63.

cratic, or at least more liberal, institutions are too well known to call for more than a passing comment in these introductory pages. Let us be content to note, for the moment, that the countries in which such dictatorships prevail today are not those in which democracy had ever firmly taken root either in the minds of the people or in the institutions of the state. Whether we consider Soviet Russia, Italy, Germany, Poland, Spain, Japan, or any of the Balkan or South American states, we find no instance of a full-fledged dictatorship succeeding a full-fledged democracy. What we do find is a sudden reversion of tendencies.

Until the World War these countries had all been subjected to the more or less autocratic rule of more or less absolute monarchs, political cliques, or individual leaders, who had never shown any true respect for the liberty and equality of the individual subject. They seemed, however, either as the result of a gradual evolution, as in Germany, Italy, and Japan, or as the consequence of a war waged to make the world safe for democracy, as in the new states, to be following the lead of the existing democracies, to be inspired by their ideals, and to be eager to emulate their institutions.

Then, almost suddenly, all these states—beginning with Russia in 1917 and ending, for the moment, with Rumania in 1938—have retraced their steps by denying their citizens the liberty and the equality they had acquired or were acquiring, by doing away with representative institutions they had enjoyed or were setting up, or by curtailing the rights which these institutions had exercised or were called upon to exercise, and by again endowing their autocratic rulers with powers which had gradually or suddenly been withdrawn from them.

It should be noted, however, that, except possibly in Japan, Jugoslavia, and Rumania, and there only with serious qualifications, these rulers were not identical with the former autocrats. While the recent establishment of dictatorships is undoubtedly a phenomenon of reaction when expressed in terms of political ideals and institutions, it is, on the contrary, heralded as a progressive movement by its promoters and its beneficiaries. And so it is, when considered from their personal point of view. Far from restoring the waning authority of former kings and emperors, the rising dictatorships have deposed or humbled them and put in their places individuals who, under the historical autocracies still more than under the short-lived pseudodemocratic regimes which temporarily succeeded them, would have been condemned to complete or at least to relative obscurity.

Under the rule of William II of Prussia or of Francis Joseph of Austria, Herr Hitler was a poor and unknown painter's apprentice. Under the more liberal institutions of the Republic of Weimar, he gradually rose to a certain prominence as a political demagogue. In the early years of the reign of Victor Emmanuel II of Savoy, Signor Mussolini was an equally obscure Italian immigrant in Switzerland. Thanks to the increasing liberalism and the gradually more comprehensive suffrage of the Italian constitution, he succeeded in becoming a socialist journalist and member of the Chamber of Deputies.

It is, therefore, not surprising that these new dictators—and the destinies of their colleagues in other countries were not dissimilar—should feel no more sympathy with their former autocratic sovereigns under whose rule they had been excluded from all influence than with the more liberal governments they had themselves overthrown, but whose liberalism alone had allowed them to gain control of their respective countries. In their own eyes they are, therefore, not reactionary enemies of liberty and equality, as one cannot but define them considering all the rights of which they have deprived their subjects—no less so because they treat them as comrades and *Volksgenossen*. In their own eyes and in their own speeches they are national heroes who have not only enhanced their countries' military power and enlarged their frontiers, but who also claim to have improved the material lot of the classes from whose ranks they have risen.

Without attempting to appraise this claim, it is

certain that the recent dictatorships, as a rule, offend far less against the principle of equality than against that of liberty. They have denied their subjects the enjoyment of practically all those rights of freedom of speech, of thought, of the press, of association, of assembly, of trade, of marriage even, which it is the boast and the honor of democratic liberalism to have introduced in the course of the nineteenth century. But as most of the dictatorships are of popular origin, they have shown themselves as hostile to all forms of hereditary social privilege and distinctions as solicitous of the material interests of the masses. Thus they have generally combated unemployment with ruthless energy and real success. They have regulated the conditions of factory labor and limited its duration as far as compatible with their ambitious programs of public works and military armaments. They have developed many useful social institutions in the interests of the health and material welfare of the working classes and particularly of their children. They have even, especially in Germany, sought to extend to certain favored representatives of the common people those joys of sport and of travel which have heretofore been the privilege of the propertied classes.

Doubtless all these measures have been inspired by considerations of political expediency—*panem ac circenses*—more than by humanitarianism. How

THE CRISIS OF DEMOCRACY

could one suspect of any feelings of humanity those whose brutality toward their political enemies knows neither bounds nor inhibitions, even when the only crime of the latter is to be of foreign blood or ancestry? However, one must recognize that throughout all their ruthless intolerance there runs a streak of popular egalitarianism. This, the dictators sometimes declare, entitles them to be considered more truly democratic than their liberal democratic foes whose political philosophy they denounce as hypocritical and repudiate as obsolete.

It is not, however, these denunciations and repudiations on the part of dictators whose countries have never known the realities of popular self-government that strike us as the most significant and alarming symptoms of the present crisis of democracy. Those symptoms we see in the difficulties inherent in the working of democracy itself under present economic, social, and international conditions.

There is, first, the difficulty of reconciling the two fundamental ideals of democracy with one another in our highly industrialized civilization. There is no doubt that the greater the measure of individual liberty maintained by the state in the modern world, the higher the degree of social inequality which will result therefrom. And, conversely, the greater the measure of equality imposed on a modern society by political authority, the narrower the margin of liberty left to the individual. In this conflict, to which we shall have occasion to revert, modern democracy is tending more and more to sacrifice liberty to equality.[9]

From the beginnings of labor legislation, which tended to limit the hours of work in factories irrespective of the wishes of both employer and employed, to the establishment of a completely planned economy, in which not only the production of wealth but also its consumption is strictly regulated at the cost of the freedom of the individual, the road is long but not very tortuous. Step by step the people—that is, the majority, that is, those who envied but did not share the ability of the best and the strongest—have used their political power to curb the initiative of the latter, thereby sacrificing liberty to equality. Doubtless, the liberty of the minority of the ablest was not sacrificed to equality alone but often also to humanity and to the social well-being of the weaker. The brakes which the will of democracy has put on the machine of production have most certainly, by regulating and by slowing down its throbbing rhythm, saved hundreds of thousands whom it would otherwise have crushed. But that undeniable fact should not

[9] Thus my lamented fellow-countryman, Professor Fleiner, could declare, not without some exaggeration to be sure: "Demokratie und individuelle Freiheit sind Gegensätze" (F. Fleiner, *Schweizerisches Bundesstaatsrecht* [Tübingen, 1923], p. 25).

blind us to the no less deniable fact that social legislation, with all the regulations it entails and all the financial burdens it imposes on production, is, and remains, a brake. By subordinating the creation of wealth to its more equal distribution, it not only tends to sacrifice the liberty of the abler few to the equality of all, but also the wealth of all to the protection of the weaker many.

Democracy would not be more faithful to its fundamental creed if it allowed its ideals of equality to be eclipsed by its ideals of liberty. Its normal development and indeed its future depend on its ability to maintain a wholesome equilibrium between the two. But majorities being what they naturally are, the dangers of their neglecting the claims of equality are far less than those of exaggerating them and of substituting the intolerance of the multitude for the liberty of all.

The second difficulty of contemporary democracy is that arising out of its relations with efficiency. In this respect, the number of sins committed in the name of liberty are hardly less than those springing from an excessive cult of equality. It is obvious that, in the long run, democracy cannot hope to prevail if it fosters inefficiency, or even if it fails to favor efficiency more than its dictatorial rivals. One of the most dangerous symptoms of the prevailing crisis of democracy is the loss of time and effort it entails. It tends to waste time and

effort in sterile political intrigues and endless irrelevant discussions often leading up to unsound
compromises or absolute deadlock, in demagogic
policies calculated to disguise the plain facts that
all monopoly, whether of capital or of labor or of
the state, reduces, and that all productive effort
increases, social welfare, in labor struggles, in
strikes, and in lockouts which benefit no one but
more reasonable competitors abroad.

It would seem that, in the long run, the efficiency
of democracy should prove superior to that of dictatorships, as liberty is more naturally productive
and inventive than oppression. But, in the short
run, may not the contrary be true? May not the
advantages of ruthlessly rational organization by
the leaders and of strict, unquestioning discipline
on the part of their followers more than outweigh
the benefits of freedom? What seems certain, in
any case, is that a regime exclusive both of individual liberty and of well-practiced discipline cannot hope to survive in the competition either with
healthy democracies or with strongly organized
dictatorships.

The third and last factor in the crisis of democracy today, we see in the international situation.

No one who has served in the army of even the
most democratic country can fail to realize that an
army is not and cannot be democratically organized if it is to fulfil its purpose. Neither defensive

nor offensive warfare can be effectively waged by an electioneering crowd. The code of war neither knows nor tolerates either liberty or equality, but only stern discipline and absolute hierarchy.

Now the state of Europe and of the world for the last twenty years has been a state of potential war more than of secure peace. It has therefore been such as to put a premium on action as opposed to discussion, on will-power as opposed to thought, and consequently on dictatorship as opposed to democracy. *Faites un roi, sinon faites la paix*— "Make a King or Make Peace"—such was the title of a book published shortly before the last war by Marcel Sembat, one of the most brilliant of French socialists of the last generation.[10] It expressed an unsavory but still a profound truth.

Democracy thrives on peace, and dictatorships on war. That is, among several others, one of the reasons why democracies tend to be pacific and dictatorships bellicose. As birds prefer the air and fish the sea, so each political regime instinctively tends toward the condition in which its virtues are most manifest and its weaknesses best disguised.

The crisis of democracy today is therefore to a large extent the crisis of world-peace.

[10] Paris, 1913.

CHAPTER II

THE RISE OF DEMOCRACY IN EUROPE

In our introductory chapter we have attempted to outline in general terms what we mean by democracy and by its present crisis. In this chapter we shall endeavor to sketch the rise of democracy in Europe from its earliest beginnings until the World War.

This inquiry is directly relevant both to our analysis of democracy and to our estimate of its crisis. It is of interest not only to the student of democracy itself because, in order to understand fully any human institution or indeed any natural phenomenon, it is always useful to discover its antecedents, its origins, and its evolution. It may also be immediately helpful for our special purposes in that it may throw some light on the crisis which democracy is undergoing today.

For anyone who would wish to form a rational judgment on the probable outcome of that crisis, it cannot be a matter of indifference either to know whether democracy has ever undergone any comparable crises in the past or to appreciate the circumstances to which the present one owes its origin. If these circumstances were accidental, one would naturally expect their consequences to partake of their accidental and therefore local and transient nature. If, on the contrary, they were of a permanent or at least of a more lasting and more general character, the chances are that the effects will survive as long as and wherever the causes to which they are to be attributed remain operative. In considering this very problem from the same point of view in his *Modern Democracies*, Lord Bryce wrote:

> This enquiry will lead us to note in each case whether the change which transferred power from the Few to the Many sprang from a desire to be rid of grievances attributed to mis-government or was created by a theoretical belief that government belonged of right to the citizens as a whole. In the former alternative the popular interest might flag when the grievances had been removed, in the latter only when the results of democratic government had been disappointing.[1]

The first question which confronts anyone who wishes to discuss, and were it only in the briefest outline, the evolution of democracy is that of the place and time of its historical origins.

For those fanatics of women's rights who deny that they ever have been or can ever be effectively represented in political society by their fathers, brothers, husbands, or sons, democracy begins in Anglo-Saxon countries on the morrow of the World War. For those enthusiasts of direct legislation for whom true democracy cannot be said to exist before the introduction of the initiative and the

[1] James Bryce, I, 27–28.

referendum, it would date from Switzerland in the middle of the last century. For those more thoughtful observers for whom the essence of democracy is to be discovered not in this or that electoral device but in the fundamental spirit and purposes of popular government, the two coasts of the North Atlantic would be places and the last quarter of the eighteenth century a time of peculiar interest.

But if, not content with noting the facts of constitutional history, we should wish to probe into the evolution of the human mind and into that of its social environment, where and when should we call a halt? In Great Britain in the seventeenth century where and when not only a few philosophers in their studies but a whole people in parliament and even on the battlefields of civil war discussed the respective rights of the one, of the few, and of the many? In the sixteenth century on the continent of Europe where the traditional authority of the Roman church was challenged in the name not of democracy, to be sure, but of ethical principles not unrelated to those from which democracy drew its most potent arguments in favor of the rights of the individual and of the fundamental equality of all human beings?

Shall we go farther still, to the Renaissance with its resurrection of classical thought, to the earliest Italian city-states with their self-willed and self-directed emancipation from feudal rulers, to the Middle Ages with their popular assemblies and their rudimentary parliaments? Or shall we leap over another millenary to the foundation of Christianity, or even over several further centuries and discover in the Athens of Pericles, if not the origins, then at least some antecedents of modern democracy which were assuredly not without influence on its re-emergence in modern times?

It would be tempting to begin this historical survey by an analysis of the Athenian democracy of the fifth century before our era. It would be tempting, not only by reason of the irresistible fascination of that incomparable epoch when humanity reached perhaps the highest peak in the whole history of its experience and accomplishments at once in the fields of art, literature, philosophy, and politics; but it would be tempting also because, in considering it in the light of its historians and philosophers, we would have before us a complete cycle of development. We would see democracy gradually emerging from the twilight of kingship and aristocracy into the radiant midday of true popular government and then slowly receding again into the darkness of subjection, mainly, it would seem, by reason of its failings in the sphere of public finance and of war.

To that double temptation, however, I shall not succumb, first, because I have neither the classical culture which would be needed to do justice to that exalted subject nor the impertinence to dispense with that culture. Furthermore, in spite of all that has been written to the contrary, I cannot but feel skeptical about the real bearing of that sublime experiment in the history of mankind on the birth, development, and crisis of modern democracy.

A city-state so small that all its citizens could be reached by the human voice in the Ecclesia, on Pnyx Hill, and that without any of our latter-day acoustic devices; a population in which a minority of free men ruled over a majority of aliens and slaves, the latter being the main substitute for our present wealth-producing and income-yielding capitalistic machinery; a civilization as exquisite in its simple refinement and as rudimentary in its economic structure as ours is crude and complicated; are not the contrasts between the world in which the Athenian Demos was king and our modern democracies too numerous and too obvious for it to be truly practicable and profitable for the latter to seek enlightenment at the school of the former?

Nevertheless, before most regretfully taking leave of the Athens of Pericles, we may be forgiven for recalling once again that immortal funeral speech in honor of those who died in the first year of the Peloponnesian War, in 431 B.C., in which that general, according to Thucydides, defined the spirit and the institutions of his own country. Let us quote from Sir Alfred Zimmern's admirable translation.

Of the battles which we and our fathers fought, whether in the winning of our power abroad or in bravely withstanding the warfare of barbarian or Greek at home, I do not wish to say more: they are too familiar to you all. I wish rather to set forth the spirit in which we faced them, and the constitution and manners with which we rose to greatness, and to pass from them to the dead; for I think it not unfitting that these things should be called to mind at today's solemnity, and expedient too that the whole gathering of citizens and strangers should listen to them.

For our government is not copied from those of our neighbours: we are an example to them rather than they to us. Our constitution is named a democracy, because it is in the hands not of the few but of the many. But our laws secure equal justice for all in their private disputes, and our public opinion welcomes and honours talent in every branch of achievement, not for any sectional reason but on grounds of excellence alone. And as we give free play to all in our public life, so we carry the same spirit into our daily relations with one another. We have no black looks or angry words for our neighbour if he enjoys himself in his own way, and we abstain from the little acts of churlishness which, though they leave no mark, yet cause annoyance to whoso notes them. Open and friendly in our private intercourse, in our public acts we keep strictly within the control of law. We acknowledge the restraint of reverence; we are obedient to whomsoever is set in authority, and to the laws, more especially to those which offer protection to the oppressed and those unwritten ordinances whose transgression brings admitted shame. Yet ours is no work-a-day city only. No other provides so many recreations for the spirit—contests and sacrifices all the year round, and beauty in our public buildings to cheer the heart and delight the eye day by day. Moreover, the city is so large and powerful that all the wealth of all the world flows in to her, so that our own Attic products seem no

more homelike to us than the fruits of the labours of other
nations.

Our military training too is different from our opponents'.
The gates of our city are flung open to the world. We prac-
tise no periodical deportations, nor do we prevent our visitors
from observing or discovering what an enemy might usefully
apply to his own purposes. For our trust is not in the devices
of material equipment, but in our own good spirits for battle.

So too with education. They toil from early boyhood in a
laborious pursuit after courage, while we, free to live and
wander as we please, march out none the less to face the self-
same dangers. . . . .

We are lovers of beauty without extravagance, and lovers
of wisdom without unmanliness. Wealth to us is not mere
material for vainglory but an opportunity for achievement;
and poverty we think it no disgrace to acknowledge but a real
degradation to make no effort to overcome. Our citizens
attend both to public and private duties, and do not allow
absorption in their own various affairs to interfere with their
knowledge of the city's. We differ from other states in regarding the man who holds aloof from public life not as "quiet"
but as useless; we decide or debate, carefully and in person,
all matters of policy, holding, not that words and deeds go
ill together, but that acts are foredoomed to failure when
undertaken undiscussed. For we are noted for being at once
most adventurous in action and most reflective beforehand.
Other men are bold in ignorance, while reflection will stop
their onset. But the bravest are surely those who have the
clearest vision of what is before them, glory and danger alike,
and yet notwithstanding go out to meet it. In doing good,
too, we are the exact opposite of the rest of mankind. We
secure our friends not by accepting favours but by doing
them. And so we are naturally more firm in our attachments:
for we are anxious, as creditors, to cement by kind offices our
relation towards our friends. If they do not respond with the
same warmness it is because they feel that their services will
not be given spontaneously but only as the repayment of a
debt. We are alone among mankind in doing men benefits,

not on calculations of self-interest, but in the fearless confidence of freedom. In a word I claim that our city as a whole is an education to Greece, and that her members yield to none, man by man, for independence of spirit, many-sidedness of attainment, and complete self-reliance in limbs and brain.

That this is no vainglorious phrase but actual fact the supremacy which our manners have won us itself bears testimony. No other city of the present day goes out to her ordeal greater than ever men dreamed; no other is so powerful that the invader feels no bitterness when he suffers at her hands, and her subjects no shame at the indignity of their dependence. Great indeed are the symbols and witnesses of our supremacy, at which posterity, as all mankind to-day, will be astonished. We need no Homer or other man of words to praise us; for such give pleasure for a moment, but the truth will put to shame their imaginings of our deeds. For our pioneers have forced a way into every sea and every land, establishing among all mankind, in punishment or beneficence, eternal memorials of their settlement.

Such then is the city for whom, lest they should lose her, the men whom we celebrate died a soldier's death: and it is but natural that all of us, who survive them, should wish to spend ourselves in her service.[2]

With President Lincoln's Gettysburg Address, with which they have often been compared, these words are doubtless the noblest which democracy has ever inspired. May that be our excuse for quoting them here.

Christianity, neither at its birth nor in its medieval doctrines, nor at its second birth in the sixteenth century, will long delay us in our quest for the beginnings of modern democracy. It is certain that Christ's teachings concerning the universal

[2] *The Greek Commonwealth* (Oxford, 1915), pp. 200 ff.

fatherhood of God, the brotherhood of all members of the human race, and the salvation of the individual soul have so profoundly altered man's conception of his destiny and of all social relations that they could not be without their effects on political evolution. It is certain also that the rapid spread of these teachings throughout the Western world was a phenomenon so far-reaching in its consequences that everything which has happened under their influence would have happened differently, if at all, without them.

It does not follow, however, that the genesis of modern democracy can be adequately explained by the rise of Christianity. The existence of democracy at least half a millenary before Christianity and the existence of Christianity for at least a millenary and a half before the appearance of any new forms of popular government are sufficient to disallow any such simple explanation.

To refuse to see in Christianity the mother of democracy is not, however, to be blind to the spiritual and historical relations between them. In his chapter on "The Mediaeval Origins of Representative Democracy," Mr. Alan F. Hattersley, the author of an excellent recent book entitled *A Short History of Democracy*, writes:

The foundations of modern society are to be traced to the early centuries of the mediaeval era. In that period, despite the turbulence and barbarity which overwhelmed western

Europe, the operation may be discerned of two new forces which were destined powerfully to transform the basis of society. The fundamental principles of Christian ethics and the political ideals of the Teutonic peoples were then super-imposed upon ancient conceptions of the state and its government. From Christianity was derived the idea of the funda-mental equality of all men, and a regard for human individual-ity, which slowly transformed slavery into serfdom, and in-sisted, within the organisation of the Church, on the in-validity of distinctions based on birth or class. Modern de-mocracy rests on the recognition of the rights of the individual. That recognition is partly derived from religion. . . . .

The ideals of freedom and self-government were promoted throughout the Middle Ages by the organisation of the Chris-tian Church. Not only did the Church emphatically proclaim the principle of the common humanity of mankind, achieving within its own ranks the social ideals of democracy. But the very existence of the Church over against the secular state safeguarded liberty by preventing the subjection of the indi-vidual to the domination of the lay government.[3]

Leaving out of account for the moment the Teu-tonic institutions of popular government to which we shall revert when considering the origins of Swiss democracy, we note that while the Christian church was undoubtedly a haven of culture, of humanity, and therefore to some feeble degree also of the rights of the individual throughout the Mid-dle Ages, its action on the formation of anything resembling democracy was negligible until the six-teenth century. From then on, however, it became decisive in the spiritual field.

[3] (Cambridge, 1930), pp. 76 ff.

Let us consider it first in Great Britain, where for over a century and a half the religious factor played havoc with the stability of all political institutions, until in 1688 it contributed to bring about that momentous revolution out of which modern democracy was to evolve as normally as the butterfly out of the caterpillar.

Throughout western Europe the kingdoms which gradually emerged toward the close of the Middle Ages were at first all in the nature of limited monarchies. They inherited from their feudal ancestry a quasi-contractual relationship which bound together the king and his people by ties of mutual rights and duties. On the Continent, by gradual encroachment, the kings came to possess all the rights, whereas their subjects were left with all the duties.

Not so in England where the seventeenth century, which in France witnessed the final triumph of royal absolutism, ended, after prolonged struggles between crown and parliament, by the unqualified victory of the latter. Why this contrast? Two main reasons have been given to explain it.

Macaulay attributed it to a geographical factor. It was to their standing armies, which the French and Spanish monarchies succeeded in raising in spite of the opposition of their respective parliaments, that they owed their emancipation from the financial tutelage in which they had at first been held by their subjects. Macaulay writes:

In England events took a different course. This singular felicity she owed chiefly to her insular situation. Before the end of the fifteenth century great military establishments were indispensable to the dignity, and even to the safety, of the French and Castilian monarchies. If either of those two powers had disarmed, it would soon have been compelled to submit to the dictation of the other. But England, protected by the sea against invasion, and rarely engaged in warlike operations on the Continent, was not, as yet, under the necessity of employing regular troops. The sixteenth century, the seventeenth century, found her still without a standing army. At the commencement of the seventeenth century political science had made considerable progress. The fate of the Spanish Cortes and of the French States General had given solemn warning to our Parliaments; and our Parliaments, fully aware of the nature and magnitude of the danger, adopted, in good time, a system of tactics which, after a contest protracted through three generations, was at length successful.[4]

Thus, in the opinion of the great liberal historian, her insular position allowed England to dispense with a standing army and her people successfully to defend their freedom against the ever threatening encroachments of her disarmed kings. Whatever the truth of this at least very plausible explanation, it is certain that to this day the British navy enjoys a popularity with the people of England which has never been extended to the army. They realize that as long as "Britannia rules the waves, ... Britons never will be

[4] *The History of England*, I, 42–43.

slaves," that is, the slaves of a foreign power, whereas there seems to subsist a lurking suspicion that large military establishments on land are less a protection against invasion from without than a menace of oppression from within.

The other factor to which the contrast between the royal absolutism on the Continent and British constitutional liberty has been attributed is of a religious nature. The Protestant reformers, Calvin no less than Luther, whatever their spiritual audacity, were never political revolutionaries. As long as they lived, they always preached and practiced obedience to the lawfully constituted authorities in secular matters. The doctrine of legitimate resistance to political tyranny formed no part of their religious creed. On the other hand, they never hesitated to place duty to God, as they conceived it, above all other human obligations. Thus, when their followers were denied the right to worship according to their faith, this higher duty inevitably brought them, sooner or later, into conflict with the political authority of the day.

Now, whereas in the Continental monarchies of France and Spain the religion of the court was always that of the overwhelming majority of the subjects, there were constant conflicts in Great Britain throughout the latter half of the sixteenth and the greater part of the seventeenth centuries between the faith of the monarch and that of important bodies of the people. Thus the Cambridge historian Figgis, discussing "Political Thought in the Sixteenth Century," after showing how "the Reformation at once expressed and intensified the belief in the inherent sanctity of civil government in the form of the Divine Right of Kings," calls attention to what he terms "the most salient fact which counteracted the evils of this theory." This most salient fact is, in his eyes, "the fortunate accident, that as a result of the movement for reform the sovereign was sometimes the adherent of a different confession to that of his subjects. But for this fact," he adds, "there could have been in the seventeenth century few relics of any form of popular liberty or of any check on monarchical tyranny."[5]

Developing the same thought toward the close of his study, Figgis writes:

Religious liberty arose, not because the sects believed in it, but out of their passionate determination not to be extinguished, either by political or religious persecution. Political liberty was born, not so much in the notions of the Independents, as in the fact that they refused to be merged in other societies. . . . . Religious liberty is rightly described as the parent of political. The forces in favour of monarchy were so strong that, apart from a motive appealing to conscience, making it a duty . . . . to resist the government, there would have been no sufficient force to withstand the tyranny of centralisation which succeeded the anarchy of feudalism. . . . . To the spiritual intensity of the Reformers and the doctrinal

[5] *The Cambridge Modern History* (Cambridge, 1907), III, 759.

exclusiveness of the Confessions—at once the highest and the lowest expressions of "the theological age"—we owe the combination of liberty with order which is our most cherished possession to-day. If much is due to the virtues of these men, something also is owing to their vices.[6]

According to this detached interpretation of the history of the Reformation, political liberty in Great Britain would owe more to the "fortunate accident" which prevented uniformity of confessional belief in England in the sixteenth and seventeenth centuries than to the characteristic features of the Protestant faith.

Other historians, as is well known, go much farther. They show that the essence of Protestantism, as a revolt against the authorities interposed between the individual believer and the object of his faith, is to make for greater spiritual freedom and, therefore, in the long run, for democracy.

Thus my revered teacher and colleague, Charles Borgeaud, of the University of Geneva, has ever since 1894, when he published his book on *The Rise of Modern Democracy in Old and New England*,[7] a work far better known in America than in Europe, often repeated his conviction that Calvinism, through John Knox in Scotland, Roger Williams in New England, and Rousseau in France, is the primary factor in the spread of democracy in the modern world.[8]

[6] *Ibid.*, pp. 768–69. [7] London.
[8] *Pages d'histoire nationale* (Geneva, 1934), pp. 122 ff.

Speculations concerning the relative importance of various factors—spiritual, intellectual, political, and economic—on the course of events are always of necessity more or less conjectural. But if opinions vary on the ingredients, there can be no discussion on the nature of the dish. It is certain that after all the turmoil of the sixteenth and seventeenth centuries the revolution of 1688 in England and the adoption of the Bill of Rights by parliament in October, 1689, definitively re-established the authority of constitutional monarchy in Great Britain and prepared the political stage for further steps toward popular government.

In "asserting the ancient rights and liberties of England," the authors of the Bill of Rights seemed to take their stand on the basis of tradition. But while denouncing past invasions of these rights and liberties, they did not fail both to confirm and to extend them. To quote Lord Acton:

> The Bill of Rights is the greatest thing done by the English nation. It established the State upon a contract, and set up the doctrine that a breach of contract forfeited the crown. . . . . Parliament gave the crown, and gave it under conditions. Parliament became supreme in administration as well as in legislation. The king became its servant on good behaviour, liable to dismissal for himself or his ministers. All this was not restitution, but inversion. Passive obedience had been the law of England. Conditional obedience and the right of resistance became the law. Authority was limited and regulated and controlled. The Whig theory of government

was substituted for the Tory theory on the fundamental points of political science.[9]

If John Locke, the most distinguished expositor of the Whig theory of government at the end of the seventeenth century, can be held to have truly interpreted it, that theory comes very near to being a philosophy of democracy. For Locke, all men are born free and equal, as he repeatedly declares[10] in formulas which were almost verbally taken over by the authors of the various declarations of rights of the American and French constitutions a century later. Furthermore, the supreme power rests with the people, that is, as he repeatedly states also, with the majority. In order to exchange the anarchy of the state of nature for the advantages and comforts of political society, the people frame a social compact.[11]

[9] *Lectures on Modern History* (London, 1926), p. 231.

[10] Thus for instance: "Man being born . . . . with a Title to perfect Freedom, and an uncontrouled enjoyment of all the Rights and Priviledges of the Law of Nature, equally with any other Man, or Number of Men in the World, hath by Nature a Power, not only to preserve his Property, that is, his Life, Liberty and Estate, against the Injuries and Attempts of other Men; but to judge of, and punish the breaches of that Law in others" (*Two Treatises of Government* [London, 1698], p. 229).

[11] "Thus every Man by consenting with others to make one Body Politick under one Government, puts himself under an Obligation to every one of that Society, to submit to the determination of the majority, and to be concluded by it; or else this original Compact, whereby he with others incorporates into one Society, would signifie nothing. . . . . For if the consent of the majority shall not in reason

By this agreement they may either retain for themselves the right to legislate and thereby constitute what Locke expressly calls a democracy,[12] or they may intrust a legislature with the exercise of this supreme power. If they adopt the latter alternative, which Locke clearly favors, they are bound to abide by the decisions of the legitimately constituted legislature.[13] But as the supreme power is transferred into the hands of the latter as a fiduciary trust only, the loyalty of the people is conditioned by the fidelity with which their legislators carry out their duty and, in particular, respect the fundamental rights of freedom and property.[14]

---

be received as the act of the whole, and conclude every individual; nothing but the consent of every individual can make any thing to be the act of the whole" (*ibid.*, pp. 239–40).

[12] "The Majority having . . . . upon Mens first uniting into Society, the whole power of the Community, naturally in them, may imploy all that power in making Laws for the Community from time to time, and Executing those Laws by Officers of their own appointing; and then the Form of the Government is a perfect Democracy" (*ibid.*, p. 265).

[13] "This Legislative is not only the supream power of the Commonwealth, but sacred and unalterable in the hands where the Community have once placed it" (*ibid.*, p. 267).

[14] "Though in a Constituted Commonwealth standing upon its own Basis, and acting according to its own Nature, that is, acting for the preservation of the Community, there can be but one Supream Power, which is the Legislative, to which all the rest are and must be subordinate, yet the Legislative being only a Fiduciary Power to act for certain ends, there remains still in the People a Supream Power to remove or alter the Legislative, when they find the Legislative act contrary to the trust reposed in them" (*ibid.*, p. 281).

As to the composition of the legislature, Locke displays a singular reticence. According to his theoretical ideals it ought to be an elected body representative of the sovereign people. As he was, however, at least as anxious to explain and to justify the Whig policy of his day as to expound an original philosophy of government, he admits that the legislature may be at least partially constituted by other methods and modified in its composition by what he calls the "Prerogative of the Prince."[15]

What remained to be done after 1689 in order to establish modern democracy in Great Britain was mainly to transform the British parliament, which, although the representative of the people as opposed to the crown, was still the organ of the landed aristocracy, into an instrument for the faithful expression of the will of the nation as a whole. In theory, that is, in Locke's theory of government, such a change was only of minor importance, since it did not involve the admission of any new fundamental principle. In practice, however, that is, in historical fact, it did imply an evolution which even today, two hundred and fifty years after the revolution of 1688, has not yet fully run its course.

For nearly a century and a half of that period no real progress toward democracy can be recorded in

[15] *Ibid.*, pp. 291.

Great Britain. It was only after the British mind
had been freed from the horror inspired by the
French Revolution that the Reform Act of 1832
could be adopted. As the wealth of the country
increased, as new classes came to be enriched and
enlightened without becoming enfranchised, as new
industrial centers were developed without receiv-
ing due representation, while old boroughs, controlled by their traditional patrons, continued to
send members to the House of Commons, time was
working against democracy more than in its favor.
The conflict thus generated between the dynamics
of social evolution and the statics of political institutions is admirably defined in the following extract from the first of the five speeches delivered
by Macaulay in the unreformed House of Commons, of which he was a member, in favor of parliamentary reform, on March 2, 1831:

We talk of the wisdom of our ancestors: and in one respect at least they were wiser than we. They legislated for
their own times. They looked at the England which was before them. They did not think it necessary to give twice as
many Members to York as they gave to London, because
York had been the capital of Britain in the time of Con-
stantius Chlorus; and they would have been amazed indeed
if they had foreseen, that a city of more than a hundred thousand inhabitants would be left without representatives in the
nineteenth century, merely because it stood on ground which,
in the thirteenth century, had been occupied by a few huts.
They framed a representative system, which, though not
without defects and irregularities, was well adapted to the
state of England in their time. But a great revolution took

place. The character of the old corporations changed. New forms of property came into existence. New portions of society rose into importance. There were in our rural districts rich cultivators, who were not freeholders. There were in our capital rich traders, who were not liverymen. Towns shrank into villages. Villages swelled into cities larger than the London of the Plantagenets. Unhappily, while the natural growth of society went on, the artificial polity continued unchanged. The ancient form of the representation remained; and precisely because the form remained, the spirit departed. Then came that pressure almost to bursting, the new wine in the old bottles, the new society under the old institutions. It is now time for us to pay a decent, a rational, a manly reverence to our ancestors, not by superstitiously adhering to what they, in other circumstances, did, but by doing what they, in our circumstances, would have done. All history is full of revolutions, produced by causes similar to those which are now operating in England. A portion of the community which had been of no account expands and becomes strong. It demands a place in the system, suited, not to its former weakness, but to its present power. If this is granted, all is well. If this is refused, then comes the struggle between the young energy of one class and the ancient privileges of another. Such was the struggle between the Plebeians and the Patricians of Rome. Such was the struggle of the Italian allies for admission to the full rights of Roman citizens. Such was the struggle of our North American colonies against the mother country. Such was the struggle which the Third Estate of France maintained against the aristocracy of birth. . . . . Such, finally, is the struggle which the middle classes in England are maintaining against an aristocracy of mere locality, against an aristocracy the principle of which is to invest a hundred drunken pot-wallopers in one place, or the owner of a ruined hovel in another, with powers which are withheld from cities renowned to the furthest ends of the earth for the marvels of their wealth and of their industry.[16]

[16] *Speeches and Legal Studies* (Fireside ed.; Boston and New York, 1910), pp. 8–9. It is interesting to note that Locke, writing before the

THE CRISIS OF DEMOCRACY

The Act of 1832, which was vigorously advocated in parliament and clamorously demanded by
the masses without, but staunchly resisted by important representatives of the privileged classes,
was by no means a radical or even a truly democratic measure. It was indeed supported by many
Liberals who, like Macaulay himself, were outspoken opponents of universal suffrage. It merely
made the House of Commons more representative
of the population, of the wealth, and of the intelligence of the country by transferring voting power
from a small minority of landowners to the urban

---

beginning of the eighteenth century, had already foreseen the need
of periodic adaptations of the system of parliamentary representation
to the changing structure of society. Compare the following extract from Locke with the above-mentioned quotation from Macaulay:

"Things of this World are in so constant a Flux, that nothing remains long in the same State. Thus People, Riches, Trade, Power
change their Stations, flourishing mighty Cities come to ruine, and
prove in time neglected desolate Corners, whilst other unfrequented
places grow into populous Countries, fill'd with Wealth and Inhabitants. But things not always changing equally, and private
interest often keeping up Customs and Priviledges when the reasons
of them are ceased, it often comes to pass that in Governments
where part of the Legislative consists of Representatives chosen by
the People, that in tract of time this Representation becomes very
unequal and disproportionate to the reasons it was at first establish'd
upon. To what gross absurdities the following of Custom when Reason
has left it may lead, we may be satisfied when we see the bare Name of
a Town, of which there remains not so much as the ruines, where scarce
so much Housing as a Sheep-coat, or more Inhabitants than a shep-
herd is to be found, sends as many Representatives to the grand
Assembly of Law-makers, as a whole Country numerous in People,
and powerful in riches" (Locke, *op. cit.*, pp. 288-89).

middle classes and to the upper section of manual laborers.

Since then over a century has passed, in the course of which, by three successive stages, in 1866, 1885, and 1918, Great Britain has extended the suffrage to the whole body of her adult resident citizens. The only obstacle which may still thwart the legislative will of the majority of the British people is today the House of Lords. But that obstacle is by no means formidable. This is so not only because the government of the day, when clearly supported by a popular majority, always has it in its power to alter that of the upper chamber by the creation of new peers, but also because that chamber, which has already been deprived of all its former rights in the field of budgetary legislation, is far too cautious to risk a serious conflict with the Commons on any other question of major policy.

That Great Britain is, politically speaking, a true democracy today, no one can deny. Nor is it ever even questioned by anyone in public life, the most conservative politicians being no less insistent than their Liberal and Labor opponents in the assertion of their democratic loyalty. But although, thanks to their political institutions, the British people can always have their way—and is there any better practical test of democracy?—that way does not lie in the direction of the abolition of either the monarchy or the aristocracy. It might even be said that the crown and the nobility are today more firmly established in democratic Great Britain than ever before, since their rights and privileges are constantly being confirmed by the freely expressed will of the people themselves.

As the progress toward the establishment of democratic institutions has been longer and more uninterruptedly continuous in Great Britain than elsewhere, so there is perhaps no country in which less is heard of the crisis of democracy today. It is interesting to note that one of the few books dealing with the topic that have appeared in England in the course of the last years has come from the brilliant and very radical pen of my friend Professor Laski. In his *Democracy in Crisis*,[17] he sees the crisis in democracy in the fact that British democracy is so conservative that it constitutes a perhaps insuperable obstacle to the peaceful realization of his socialistic ideals.

Nothing is historically more instructive than a comparison between the just outlined evolution in England and that by which France came to adopt her present democratic institutions. The British evolution is the story of a childhood love developing through a long, even if sometimes stormy, courtship into a steady and durable legitimate

[17] London, 1933.

union in which a deep and reasonable mutual af-
fection more than makes up for the lack of any
passionate enthusiasm. The capricious and intermittent amours of France and democracy, on the
other hand, make a very different tale, more dramatic, to be sure, but hardly as reassuring in its
outlook on the future happiness and mutual contentment of this inconstant couple.

The seventeenth century, which, as we have
seen, was in England that of the Bill of Rights,
after having been for a brief spell that of the republican Commonwealth of Oliver Cromwell, was in
France *le siècle de Louis XIV*, that is, the century
of triumphant and undisputed royal absolutism.
The personal totalitarianism of the *Roi-Soleil*, so
well defined in the formula *l'Etat c'est moi*, commonly attributed to him, was exclusive not only
of all democracy, but also of every kind of popular
control. The French States-General, of which the
British equivalent had in 1689 become the chief
power in the state, were never even summoned
from 1614 to 1789.

When they met in the spring of the latter year
and soon became the National Constituent Assembly, their intentions were by no means clear
and definite. As Aulard has conclusively shown in
the first chapter of his *Histoire politique de la
Révolution française*,[18] there were no real democrats

[18] Paris, 1905.

and no true republicans among the first revolutionary legislators of France. The general hope was that the king would protect his subjects against all the influences and agencies which were responsible for a material oppression which had become intolerable. A further hope and expectation were that in that effort he would in future call on the support of all his people more than on his past advisers. But while a limited monarchy something on the model of the British seemed to be the general constitutional ideal of the majority, the authority of the crown was in fact far more deeply undermined than was clearly realized either by Louis XVI or by any of his critics in 1789.

A king, both as the object of the veneration of his subjects and as the source of political power, may rely either on their traditional loyalty based on the long recollection of services rendered, of common sufferings and of common glories shared in the past, or he may rely on a general religious faith in his divine right, or he may, in the last resort, rely on an overwhelming force. The French throne, which had under Louis XIV been solidly set up and maintained on this triple foundation, had been badly shaken in the course of the eighteenth century.

Of traditional loyalty, there remained, it is true, some appearance. When Louis XVI appeared before the assembled States-General in Versailles on

May 4 and May 5, 1789, he met with an enthusiastic and almost ecstatic reception. The crowd
reserved all their applause for his royal person and
for the representatives of the Third Estate,
whereas they showed an equally marked coolness
on the passage of the queen, the princes, the nobility, and the clergy. It almost seemed as if the
king was expected to save his miserable people
from his own surroundings. It soon became evident, however, that no matter how sincerely
Louis XVI may have desired the happiness of all
his subjects and the abolition of all abusive and
oppressive practices, he would side with those who
had traditionally been his companions and advisers
if and when called upon to choose between them
and the masses. The glory of the *Roi-Soleil* was
no more. What remained in the heart of the people
was the bitterness engendered by all the abuses
and injustices which they had suffered as well as
by all the scandals which they had witnessed.
When the hope that the king was ready and able
to effect a radical reform and to restore the rights
of man came to be disappointed, as it was very
shortly, then, but then only, republican and democratic measures came to be considered.

As for religious belief in the divine origin of kingship, it is of course impossible to estimate how
much of it remained vital in the soul of the common
Frenchman. What is certain is that in the minds

of the enlightened middle-class leaders it had not survived a century of rationally superficial but sarcastically brilliant and utterly destructive metaphysical literature. Never had the intellectual prestige of the pen stood higher in France than during the age of the so-called "philosophers." Although illiteracy was still rampant among the rural masses, these authors were acclaimed by an ever widening audience among the rising bourgeoisie, and it was the latter who, voicing and thereby exciting the discontent of the former and of the urban populace, were to overthrow the French monarchy.

To military force, the last prop of the French throne, Louis XVI did in fact appeal on various occasions, but never with success. As early as the beginnings of July, 1789, the National Assembly asked the king to withdraw the mercenary foreign troops which had been assembled around Versailles and were threatening its free intercourse with Paris. The king refused. Paris rose, the Bastille was taken on July 14, 1789, and the Assembly was freed. The significance of this event is shown by the fact that republican France has chosen this date for its national holiday.

On August 4, the king was by decree of the Assembly declared to be "the restorer of the liberty of France," but in fact he was coming to be considered and treated as the first public servant of the nation and no longer obeyed as its absolute ruler. By a subsequent decree of August 14, a new oath of loyalty was administered to the officers and men of the army, according to which they were to swear fidelity to "the nation, the king and the law," in that order. By this decree the power of the sword was divorced from the authority of the crown.

From this time on the king was the prisoner of the nation. When, on October 5, 1789, he had first refused to accept the Declaration of Rights and the Constitution providing for a limited monarchy, which the National Assembly had adopted, he was brought from Versailles to Paris. When over a year and a half later, on June 21, 1791, he sought to flee over the borders of his country with the intention of returning at the head of an army of aristocratic *émigrés*, he was caught and brought back from Varennes to Paris under military escort and put back on his constitutional throne against his will. When in April, 1792, war broke out between revolutionary France, of which Louis XVI was still the monarch, and her Austro-Prussian enemies, with whom he secretly sympathized, the king of the French was deprived of his bodyguard. Finally, on August 10, 1792, when the armed populace of Paris and of the provinces had overcome the resistance of Louis XVI's last defenders, his faithful Swiss regiments, the throne was declared va-

cant and shortly after its last incumbent was condemned to death and executed.

Thus, in the brief space of three years, the successor of Louis XIV had lost with his last hold on
the loyalty of his subjects his last means of co-
ercing them by force. The stage was accordingly
set for the rise of republican democracy in France.

France, which had been unanimously monarchical even after acclaiming the Declaration of
Rights in 1789, had, in 1792, become republican
as the result of the hesitations and then of the
treason of her last king. Furthermore, the real
power in the state had passed from the bourgeoisie,
represented by the National Assembly, to the
masses. This transfer of power brought with it a
fundamental change. It implied that the newly established republic was to be truly democratic.
The constitution which had been adopted in 1789
on the basis of the rights of man had, by restricting the suffrage to property owners, secured the
rule of the middle classes. As in England a century before and as only a few years previously in
America, it had not been deemed inconsistent first
to proclaim that all men were born free and equal
and then to exclude the majority from all active
citizenship. But, as in England and in America
also, logic could not fail in the end to prevail over
expediency. In France, however, its triumph was
much more rapid, but correspondingly less lasting.

DEMOCRACY IN EUROPE

It hardly took France more years than it took
Great Britain centuries and the United States
decades to pass from the theoretical assertion of
liberty and equality as political ideals to the adoption of universal, by which was meant manhood,
suffrage as a practical means of realizing those
ideals. But whereas in the Anglo-Saxon communities manhood and then universal suffrage, once
established, have never been challenged, the constitution of June 24, 1793, the most democratic
ever adopted in France, never came into force. Its
promulgation having been retarded by reason of
foreign and civil wars, it was in 1795 superseded
by the fundamental law of the Republic of Ven-
démiaire 1st, Year IV. After many allusions in the
debates to the wisdom of the Americans, who had
recognized that the ownership of property was a
necessary condition for the exercise of the rights
of citizenship, universal suffrage was replaced by
electoral rights limited to a well-defined class of
taxpayers.[19]

But even with this important qualification, not
only the practice but even the theory of democratic
government in France was soon to undergo a long
eclipse. This eclipse lasted for more than half a
century and then, after a reviving flash in 1848,
for another twenty years. Neither under Napoleon
Bonaparte as consul, nor under Napoleon I as

[19] *Ibid.*, p. 550.

emperor, nor under Louis XVIII and Charles X after the Restoration, nor under Louis-Philippe after the revolution of 1830, nor after that of 1848 under Napoleon the president and then the emperor, in spite of his plebiscites, was France either a republic or a democracy.

She became both after her defeat at the hands of Germany in 1871, and she has remained both before, during, and after her victory over Germany in 1918. For over sixty years, that is, for a period far longer than the duration of any of her previous regimes since her first revolution, France has now been true to the same fundamental institutions. Is her faith in them still unshaken today? It would be rash to assert it after all her post-war disappointments. What is unshaken in contemporary France, however, is the aversion of the majority of her people to either of her past royal or imperial absolutisms or to anything resembling the dictatorships of Italy or Germany. They may be tired of her present party system and of the financial failings of her present rulers, but they are not as yet prepared to purchase more order, stricter economy, and greater efficiency at the price of less liberty and more inequality.

In this hasty sketch of the rise of democracy in Europe, we have dealt with Great Britain and France first. We have done so because they are the only two democratic great powers in the Old World today and because we are here concerned with the past only in so far as it allows us to understand the present and, if possible, to foresee the future. Had we been studying the past for the past's sake, we would have had ample excuse for following our own natural inclination and for beginning our historical survey with Switzerland.

It was not one of my fellow-countrymen, but Lord Bryce himself, who declared, in the opening words of his *Modern Democracies:*

A century ago there was in the Old World only one tiny spot in which the working of democracy could be studied. A few of the ancient rural cantons of Switzerland had recovered their freedom after the fall of Napoleon, and were governing themselves as they had done from the earlier Middle Ages. . . . . Nowhere else in Europe did the people rule.[20]

The fact cannot be disputed, although its influence on the rise of modern democracy may well be and has often been misunderstood and exaggerated. The three mountain cantons around the Lake of Lucerne, in the heart of the Alps, have often been called the cradle of European democracy, as they undoubtedly are the cradle of the independent statehood of Switzerland. What is the truth and what the significance of the emergence and continuous existence for over six centuries of self-governing institutions in these Alpine communities?

[20] I, 3.

THE CRISIS OF DEMOCRACY

In the earliest times of our era there was a tradition and a practice of self-government among the free men of Europe. It was to this tradition and to this practice that Mr. Hattersley was referring when, in the above-quoted passage, he spoke of "the political ideals of the Teutonic peoples." The rights of popular assemblies, which were always asserted in the course of the development of the British monarchy, generally disappeared elsewhere. They did not, as a rule, survive the rise of feudalism and the rise of kingship.

In the Alps, however, geography, combined with the spirit of independence and the military prowess it engendered among their inhabitants, allowed the free men of Uri, Schwytz, and Unterwalden to remain their own masters throughout the centuries. And so it came about that these three cantons and three others who later joined with them and with their first urban allies spoke of themselves and especially were described by foreign observers as democracies. Thus, for instance, the Rev. William Coxe, perhaps the best informed of all the British tourists who visited Switzerland in the last quarter of the eighteenth century, commonly spoke of the six "democratical" cantons.[21]

The three above-mentioned cantons as well as Zoug, Appenzell, and Glarus, assuredly deserved

[21] *Travels in Switzerland* (4th ed.; 3 vols.; London, 1801), I, 43, 257, 299.

the name because, according to their form of government, supreme power was vested in the whole adult body of the citizens. Annually these citizens met in open-air assemblies, called *Landsgemeinde*, in which each had an equal vote and there elected their magistrates and adopted their laws.

In spite of the clearly democratic character of these institutions, however, they appear almost as foreign to modern democracies as does the Athenian Republic of the fifth century B.C. As in Athens, the rights of citizenship were denied to all aliens and reserved to the families of local stock, who, at the end of the *ancien régime*, were far outnumbered by those of their subjects within and without their borders. Far more than in Athens, there prevailed in these Alpine democracies a spirit of narrow intolerance. This spirit rendered them passionately hostile, not only to the French Revolution and to its principles of liberty and equality, but also to the rise of modern democracy in the neighboring Swiss cantons after 1830. Thanks mainly to the dominant influence of the Roman Catholic clergy, an influence favored more than restricted by their institutions of voting in public, they stubbornly opposed the introduction of the federal constitution of 1848, which made of Switzerland the truly democratic country which she is today.

THE CRISIS OF DEMOCRACY

It must be admitted—although I do so not without reluctance—that all the economic, social, and intellectual changes which have made for modern democracy in Switzerland and in the rest of the world have proved contrary to the survival of these traditional forms of self-government which, accordingly, tend more and more to disappear. While the admirers and representatives of these institutions were therefore quite consistent in viewing these changes with suspicion and hostility, it is obviously impossible to maintain without serious qualification the myth of the Swiss *Landsgemeinde* as the embryo of European democracy today.

It is true, however, that, surrounded on all sides by the monarchical absolutism which obtained all over the continent of Europe before the French Revolution, Switzerland enjoyed and deserved the reputation of being the home of a relatively free people. In the first place, she had never, since the earliest alliances between the three primitive cantons in 1291 until the formation of the Confederacy of the thirteen cantons, of which she was composed at the end of the eighteenth century, been anything but a federation of republican states. Except for the six Alpine democracies, all these states, the most important of which were Berne and Zurich, were urban aristocracies or oligarchies which ruled over relatively large rural provinces and in which the powers of government were vested in a limited number of privileged families. As, in the course of the centuries, the number of these families had been decreasing, the political regime in Switzerland was becoming ever less democratic when, in 1798, it was violently upset from without as a result of the French Revolution. Still the republican pluralistic form of government in which the hereditary principle was always tempered by elections, the absence of any national standing army, the relative material welfare and intellectual enlightenment of the mass of the people combined with the small size of the cantons and the extensive practice of municipal and communal autonomy, all tended to maintain a general state of political liberalism very different from that prevailing in the neighboring monarchies.

It is on the basis of this liberal tradition in the urban cantons much more than on that of the Alpine democracies, that modern self-governing institutions were built up in Switzerland in the nineteenth century.[22] Modern democracy in the Swiss cantons may be dated from the morrow of the July revolution of 1830 in Paris. It was when the citizens of the large cantons realized that the Holy Alliance was unwilling or unable to defend by force the reactionary institutions which had been

[22] I have discussed this topic rather thoroughly in my book on *L'Individu et l'Etat dans l'évolution constitutionnelle de la Suisse* (Zurich, 1936), and more summarily in my *Government of Switzerland* (New York, 1936).

set up under its influence in 1815, that they revolted against them. As a consequence of a series
of local bloodless revolutions, all the more important Swiss cantons were, in 1830 and 1831, endowed with new constitutions under which the
will of the majority was bound to prevail. In 1848,
after a brief civil war, a federal constitution was
adopted which, while respecting the essential autonomy of the cantons, extended to all the fundamental principles of political liberalism which had
triumphed in the more advanced communities in
1830.

Since then and until the World War, the political
evolution in Switzerland has been in the direction
of ever greater and truer democracy. The initiative, the referendum, and proportional representation, which were adopted first in the cantons and
then in the federal state, were nothing but means
devised to secure a fuller and ever more faithful
expression of the will of the people. Since the
World War, as we shall see when dealing with the
crisis of democracy, a slight reaction has been
noticeable. It is by no means such, however, as to
preclude us from counting Switzerland among the
states in which modern democracy is most firmly
established and most consistently practiced today.

The fact that the Swiss people, that is, the majority of the women of Switzerland no less than
that of their male companions are still opposed to

female suffrage, much as we regret it, does not lead us seriously to qualify the foregoing statement. I have it on the authority of the leaders of the women-suffrage movement of Switzerland, that it is the women and not the men who are their most dangerous opponents. Now, if the majority of the women do really not want the ballot, it would hardly be democratic on the part of the men to impose it upon them!

Lord Bryce, writing in 1921, counted eleven democratic governments in Europe.[23] They were, besides those of the three countries we have just considered, those of the three Scandinavian states, Holland, Belgium, Portugal, Greece, and Italy. Were he writing today he would doubtless drop the last three countries from his list and probably add to it Finland and Czechoslovakia.

In any case, democratic governments, although they have always been in a minority on the continent of Europe, are still too numerous to allow us in the brief space of a chapter to consider their beginnings here. Rather let us conclude by three general observations which seem to apply to all of them.

In the first place, it seems obvious that economic change in general and the industrial revolution of the nineteenth century in particular have every-

[23] *Op. cit.*, I, 26.

where tended to promote the rise and progress of democracy. By enriching and enlightening new individuals and new social classes and by concentrating populations in large urban centers they have been as a challenge to the traditional authority both of absolute monarchs and especially of the landed aristocracy. In some cases, as in Great Britain and to a lesser degree in pre-war Germany, the latter have been wise enough to associate the beneficiaries of the economic changes with their inherited power and thus to consolidate it. In other cases, as in France, it has been wrested from them. But everywhere, economic change, which in modern Europe is almost synonymous with industrialization, has made for political change, and political change has generally been in the direction of democracy. Other things being equal, it is, therefore, in the most highly industrialized states that the progress of democracy was most advanced before the World War.

Second, the progress of democracy has everywhere been promoted by peace and impeded by war. It is assuredly no accident that most of the European pre-war democracies were states whose policies had allowed them to hold aloof from the major international conflicts of the nineteenth century, or whose geographical position had at least spared them the ordeal of foreign invasion. To what seems to be a general rule, France appears to offer the one great exception. But that this exception is more apparent than real will be readily admitted by anyone familiar with recent French political history.

Finally, it may be noted that none of those states which in the nineteenth century had been led by a gradual process of evolution to adopt democratic institutions and in which such institutions had been working and developing normally for several generations have heretofore fallen a prey to post-war dictators. As we shall see more clearly in our later chapters, but as this historical sketch has already allowed us to foresee, it is not the states in which democracy was an inheritance of the past, but those in which it was merely a program or a hope for the future, that have until today succumbed to the onslaught of authoritarian violence.

CHAPTER III

THE WORLD WAR AND THE FATE
OF DEMOCRACY

The outbreak of the World War in August, 1914, was bound to have a profound effect on the fate of democracy in Europe and in the whole world. This effect, which was far from simple and indeed in some respects would seem to have been self-contradictory, we propose in this chapter to discuss under the following three headings: the war and the eclipse of democratic liberty; the war, a democratic crusade; and finally, the war and its democratic repercussions on the constitutional development of Europe.

A war, as every other serious crisis which calls for strong, ruthless, and immediate action on the part of the state, cannot fail to challenge the fundamental principles of democracy. If such action is to be taken by the government in accordance with the demands of efficiency, what will become of the rights of the citizen to be consulted beforehand and to be protected against any invasion of his constitutionally guaranteed liberties? If, on the other hand, liberties are to be respected, how can the government hope successfully to cope with the arising and constantly renewed emergencies? As

Sir Cecil Spring Rice, the British ambassador to the United States, wrote to a friend in England on September 24, 1914: "The question is, is freedom strong enough to defend itself? A government is either too strong for the freedom of its own people, or too weak to defend them from a foreign enemy."[1]

During the war, in all democratic countries, neutral as well as belligerent, this problem was solved by the deliberate provisional subordination of the freedom of the citizen to the strength of the government, that is, by an eclipse of democratic liberty. This eclipse was effected by a variety of strikingly similar devices. This similarity is all the more interesting, as it clearly resulted not from any mutual imitation but merely from the impact of the same necessities on analogous institutions. The examples given below are drawn only from the wartime experience of Great Britain, France, and Switzerland, the three states in which we have considered the beginnings of democracy. But if space permitted, similar illustrations could readily be quoted from all the other democratic governments.

In the first place, there was everywhere a tremendous concentration of power in the hands of the executive. In some countries, as in Switzer-

---

[1] *The Letters and Friendships of Sir Cecil Spring Rice*, ed. Stephen Gwynn (2 vols.; London, 1929), II, 212.

land, this was effected by a formal legislative delegation. On July 31, 1914, the Federal Council (the Cabinet) summoned the Federal Assembly (the Congress) to meet in extraordinary session and laid before it a draft bill demanding for itself full powers for the duration of the war. After a very brief debate, such powers were, on August 3, 1914, granted by a federal decree of which the following are the relevant clauses:

ART. 3. The Federal Assembly grants the Federal Council unlimited powers to take all necessary measures to insure the security, integrity and neutrality of Switzerland and to safeguard the credit and the economic interests of the country and in particular its food supply.

ART. 4. For this purpose unlimited financial credits are granted the Federal Council. It is expressly authorized to raise the necessary loans.

ART. 5. The Federal Council shall render account to the Federal Assembly at its next session of the use made of the unlimited powers hereby granted.[2]

In pursuance of this decree, the Federal Council, in the course of the World War, took over a thousand executive decisions which, under the federal constitution, should normally have been sanctioned by a previous parliamentary vote, and some of which at least should have been furthermore submitted to the referendum of the people. It could easily be argued, and in fact it could not be denied,

---

[2] Herbert Tingsten, *Les pleins pouvoirs*, trans. from the Swedish (Paris, 1934), p. 62.

that, in granting these unlimited legislative powers to the government, the Federal Assembly had acted *ultra vires*. Not only had parliament dispossessed itself of its legislative function, for which there is no express provision in the federal constitution, but it had further endowed the government with rights which it did not itself possess. The legislative act of August 3, 1914, in fact, transformed Switzerland from a constitutional democracy into a complete temporary dictatorship. This was all the more striking, as the composition of the federal government was not modified, although the Socialist party was not represented in it.

It is hardly necessary to recall that the Federal Council in no way abused the abnormal dictatorial powers with which it had been unconstitutionally vested. Not only did it faithfully present a full account of its administration to parliament at each successive session, but it constantly submitted to the Federal Assembly important measures which it preferred not to take without express legislative approval. It even organized three popular referendum votes during the war, because, in spite of its full powers, it wisely wished to associate the electorate in the responsibilities of government.

In France, where parliament was sitting when the war broke out, it never granted the executive any such full powers. It, in fact, expressly refused to do so when, in the autumn of 1916, a cabinet, presided over by M. Briand, laid before it a bill to that effect.[3]

However, by a series of special acts, of which the first, relating to finance and to the freedom of the press, were adopted without discussion on August 4, 1914,[4] the government was from time to time endowed with quasi-legislative powers and in certain cases even exercised such powers without the express previous approval of the legislature.

On the whole, nevertheless, the French chambers throughout the war showed great vigilance in their control over the government's policies. This is the more noteworthy, as from the outset the opposition had been admitted to executive responsibility in France,[5] and as none of the successive ministries which administered the country from 1914 to 1918 were strictly party governments.

In Great Britain parliament was also in session at the outbreak of the war, the Liberal government headed by Mr. Asquith being supported therein by a solid parliamentary majority. This circumstance, however, did not relieve its chief of the necessity of first asking for exceptional powers and

[3] *Ibid.*, pp. 19 ff.

[4] Raymond Poincaré, *Au service de la France* (Paris, 1927), IV, 547.

[5] *Ibid.* (Paris, 1928), V, 164 ff.

later of reconstructing his cabinet in order to broaden its parliamentary and national basis.[6]

In accordance with British traditions, the government did not, as in Switzerland, expressly request parliament to suspend in favor of the executive its normal legislative functions. But the same end was attained by a series of special measures. In the first place, beginning with August 4, 1914, the king issued a royal proclamation which was worded as follows:

Whereas by the law of Our Realm it is Our undoubted prerogative and the duty of all Our loyal subjects acting in Our behalf in times of imminent national danger to take all such measures as may be necessary for securing the public safety and the defence of Our Realm:

And whereas the present state of public affairs in Europe is such as to constitute an imminent national danger:

Now, therefore, We strictly command and enjoin Our subjects to obey and conform to all instructions and regulations which may be issued by Us or Our Admiralty or Army Councils, or any officer of Our Navy or Army, or any other person acting in Our behalf for securing the objects aforesaid, and not to hinder or obstruct, but to afford all assistance in their power to any person acting in accordance with any such instructions or regulations or otherwise in the execution of any measures duly taken for securing those objects.[7]

In spite of its general wording, this proclamation was not construed as an assertion by the crown of any unlimited powers of government. It was not

[6] The Earl of Oxford and Asquith, *Memories and Reflections* (2 vols.; London, 1928), II, 95 ff.

[7] Tingsten, *op. cit.*, pp. 178–79.

intended to withdraw from parliament either its power of the purse or any of its other legislative authority. Shortly after, beginning on August 8, a series of further measures were taken which culminated in the Defense of the Realm Consolidation Act of November 27, 1914, of which the main provisions were the following:

His Majesty in Council has power during the continuance of the present war to issue regulations for securing the public safety and the defence of the realm, and as to the powers and duties for that purpose of the Admiralty and Army Council and of the members of His Majesty's forces and other persons acting in his behalf; and may by such regulations authorize the trial by courts-martial, or in the case of minor offences by courts of summary jurisdiction, and punishment of persons committing offences against the regulations and in particular against any of the provisions of such regulations designed—

a) To prevent persons communicating with the enemy or obtaining information for that purpose or any purpose calculated to jeopardise the success of the operations of any of His Majesty's forces or the forces of his allies or to assist the enemy; or

b) to secure the safety of His Majesty's forces and ships and the safety of any means of communication and of railways, ports, and harbours; or

c) to prevent the spread of false reports or reports likely to cause disaffection to His Majesty or to interfere with the success of His Majesty's forces by land or sea or to prejudice His Majesty's relations with foreign powers; or

d) to secure the navigation of vessels in accordance with directions given by or under the authority of the Admiralty; or

e) otherwise to prevent assistance being given to the enemy or the successful prosecution of the war being endangered.[8]

[8] *Ibid.*, p. 184.

Although here again the powers granted to the king in Council, which in fact was the government of the day, might seem unlimited, the Act was always construed in a rather restrictive sense. While it did infringe on the traditional rights of the subjects of the crown—in subsequent judicial proceedings a judge declared that by reason of this Act "Magna Charta has not remained untouched"[9] —it did not entail any appreciable diminution of the rights of parliament.

The latter were, in constitutional practice, much more severely diminished by the grant of a vote of credit of £100,000,000 by the House of Commons on August 7, 1914. In proposing this vote, Mr. Asquith had declared:

As a rule in the past Votes of this kind have been taken simply for naval and military operations, but we have thought it right to ask the Cummittee to give us its confidence in the extension of the traditional area of Votes of Credit, so that this money which we are asking them to allow us to expend may be applied not only for strictly naval and military operations but to assist the food supplies, promote the continuance of trade, industry, business, and communications, whether by means of insurance, indemnity against risk or otherwise, for the relief of distress, and generally for all expenses arising out of the existence of a state of war. I believe the Committee will agree with us that it was wise to extend the area of the Vote of Credit so as to include all these serious matters. It gives the Government a free hand. Of course, the Treasury will account for it, and any expenditure that takes place will be subject to the approval of the House. I think it would be a

[9] *Ibid.*, p. 193.

great pity, in fact a great disaster, if in a crisis of this magnitude we were not enabled to make provision—provision far more needed now than it was under the simpler conditions that prevailed in the old days—for all the various ramifications and developments of expenditure which the existence of a state of war between the Great Powers of Europe must entail on any one of them.[10]

In Great Britain the constitutional concentration of responsibility and power was perhaps carried farther than in any other country. Not only did parliament—without ceasing to exercise a very vigilant supervision over the general course of affairs—give the government an extremely free hand, not only did the ministry, as is customary in Great Britain, remain under the control of the inner circle called the cabinet, but the cabinet itself was held to be too large a body effectively to deal with the conduct of the war. It was on this question and on Lloyd George's ambition to lead a small "War Committee" under the cabinet but without the chairmanship of the prime minister, that Mr. Asquith resigned on December 5, 1916.[11]

The reconstructed government under Mr. Lloyd George was headed by a so-called war cabinet, the first of which consisted of only five members under

[10] *Speeches by the Earl of Oxford and Asquith* (New York, 1927), p. 199.

[11] The Earl of Oxford and Asquith, *op. cit.*, II, 130 ff. J. A. Spender and C. Asquith, *Life of Herbert Henry Asquith* (2 vols.; London, 1932), II, 252 ff. David Lloyd George, *War Memoirs* (London, 1933), II, 979 ff.

the chairmanship of the prime minister. When the latter was forming his government, his intention had been to restrict its membership to four. Questioned by the representatives of labor, whose support he hoped to secure, as to whether "the proposed new cabinet of four members would mean that we should have four dictators," he made the following reply—equally characteristic of his own temperament and of the necessities of democratic government under war conditions:

> What is a Government for except to dictate? If it does not dictate, it is not a Government, and whether it is four or twenty-three, the only difference is that four would take less time than twenty-three. . . . . The only reason for cutting the Cabinet down to four was because with a larger number of people it meant so many men, so many minds; so many minds, so many tongues; so many tongues, so much confusion; so much confusion, so much delay.[12]

Besides this abnormal concentration of power in the hands of the executive, the war brought about a second and still more far-reaching change in the structure and working of democracy. Under the pressure of military necessity the sphere of state enterprise in economic matters was tremendously enlarged and the action of government control considerably expanded and intensified. The importance of this consequence of the war can hardly be overestimated, since it was limited neither to democratic countries, in space, nor to the duration

[12] Lloyd George, *ibid.* (London, 1934), III, 1060.

of the hostilities, in time. It involved a complete and perhaps a lasting breach with the tradition of liberal individualism under which Europe had made such gigantic strides both in wealth and in freedom in the course of the preceding century.

When and where the main function of the state is to enhance material prosperity, it wisely refrains from unduly interfering with the private activities of the individual. In this the teachings of economic liberalism have been largely confirmed by historical experience. But these teachings were based on the assumption of peaceful international relations.

When and where, on the contrary, the main function of the state is to win a war or to protect its citizens from the consequences of war, then there is hardly a sphere in which government intervention may not become a necessity. Production, trade, and even consumption must be regulated with a view not to increase the national income and individual welfare but to save the life of the national community.

It was, therefore, not only natural but perfectly legitimate that during the war the rights of the individual should everywhere have been drastically curtailed. What he was to do, with whom he was to trade, where he was to live, and how much he was to eat, were all decided for him by the state.

In this respect, more still than with regard to the

increase of executive power, the war transformed all democracies into dictatorships. And if today, twenty years after the end of the last war and—who can tell?—perhaps on the eve of another bloody catastrophe, dictatorship is rampant and democracy in crisis, it is due more than to any other single cause to the fact that the peoples of the world are being governed not so that they may be happy, prosperous, and free, but that their nations may be strong and safe.

The eclipse of democratic liberty which resulted from these interventionist policies was the more complete and the more general, as all the democratic governments were led by the same military necessities to limit the political and intellectual no less than the economic freedom of their people. This was a third general consequence of the war impeding the normal working of democracy.

That no elections could well be held while the troops were at the front was obvious even to the most convinced democrat. Even in Great Britain, where, ever since the seventeenth century, public opinion is particularly sensitive in such matters, the general elections, which were due in December, 1915, were postponed until the end of the war. As Mr. Asquith wrote in his *Memories and Reflections:*

The House of Commons had been elected in December, 1910, and as its term was limited by the Parliament Act to five years, it would if its life were prolonged to the last legal

moment expire in December, 1915. It was obviously in the
general interest highly undesirable that the country, which
was straining every nerve to ensure an effective prosecution
of the War, should be distracted by being called upon in
such conditions to prepare for and in a few months to confront
the turmoil of a general election. Accordingly it was determined by the Cabinet early in April, 1915, to communicate
with the leaders of the Opposition as to the expediency of
postponing registration and the dissolution for another year.[13]

Thus denied the right to vote, the citizens of all
democracies were also, as a result of the war, deprived of the right of free speech, almost of free
thought, and in certain cases even of the constitutional safeguards in judicial matters. The British
Defence of the Realm Act, which we quoted above
as illustrating the extension of executive power,
may be taken also as an example of legislative interference with the normal rights of free citizenship.

In all countries, democratic as well as autocratic, neutral as well as belligerent, a strict censorship was exercised over all private communications by mail and by wire as well as over the press.
Thus it became impossible for public opinion, that
fundamental basis of all free government, both to
assert itself and to be enlightened. Not only was it
denied access to the sources of real knowledge, but
it was, by the activities of government propaganda
offices, constantly being supplied with facts which
were sometimes palpably untrue and almost al-

[13] II, 23.

ways incomplete and misleadingly presented. Although this process of restricting the flow and of
poisoning the source of public information was
never carried as far in the democratic countries
during the war as it was then and again is today
in the dictatorial states, it did grievously interfere
with the normal working of free institutions. Moreover, it bred habits of reticence if not of mendacity
in government circles and habits of skepticism if
not of incredulity in the public, which are not without their influence on the crisis of democracy in
the world at large today.

For all these reasons and by all these methods—
the increase of executive authority, the extension
of state enterprise, and the restrictions on individual liberty—the World War not only played
havoc with democracy from 1914 to 1918 but
seriously jeopardized its subsequent development.

At the same time, the friends of political freedom
should be the last to overlook the no less important
fact that the World War promoted and exalted the
ideals of democracy as no event in the history of
mankind had ever done before.[14]

When the armies of the Austro-German allies
invaded Serbia, Belgium, and France, in the summer of 1914, it struck all the democratic peoples of

[14] Cf. Bourquin, "The Crisis of Democracy," in *The World Crisis*
(London, 1938), p. 67.

the world as a challenge not only to international justice and peace but also to political freedom. Without wishing to reopen once more the abominable war-guilt problem, we must recall three pertinent facts: neither France nor Great Britain nor Belgium were in 1914 aggressive nations seeking for a modification of their frontiers at the expense of their neighbors; in spite of their ominous czarist ally, they were the outstanding free peoples of Europe; their Austro-German foes were the enemies of international stability no less than of political liberty. We must recall these three major facts because they alone explain why, from the very outset, the World War appeared to millions of individuals, neutrals and belligerent, soldiers and civilians alike, as an attack on and a defense of democracy, why, after the downfall of czarism and the entrance of the United States into the conflict, it came to be regarded by them as a true crusade for democracy, and why, finally, the triumph of the Allies was the signal of a general conversion to republican democracy on the part of the defeated powers, as well as on that of those nations which their defeat had freed from their former masters.

We now propose briefly to outline this evolution of the political significance of the war in the light of contemporary comment.

Thus considered, the war naturally falls into two periods, before and after the spring of 1917, when the ghost of czarism vanished from the battlefields of Europe and when the American crusaders for democracy appeared on the scene.

At the very outset of the war all responsible statesmen of course viewed it primarily, and most of them exclusively, from the standpoint of the national interest of their respective countries. Austria-Hungary wished to punish Serbia in whom she saw an obstacle to her expansion in the Balkans and perhaps a threat to her own territorial integrity. Russia refused to submit to the renewed loss of prestige which the abandonment of her weaker Slav friend would have entailed. Germany stood by her Austro-Hungarian ally with the will to assert herself as the first military power on the Continent and in the hope of breaking the circle of suspicious neighbors by whom she declared to be threatened and who undoubtedly stood in the way of her territorial and colonial expansion. France, even had she been so inclined, could not have abandoned her Russian ally without loss of dignity, security, and even territorial integrity. As for Serbia and Belgium, they were so stunned by the blow of invasion that their only thought was for their own national existence.

Of all the states that were to become the first European belligerents, Great Britain alone could and did in the early days of August, 1914, look beyond her most immediate national interests. She obviously had no aggressive designs. She was bound by no military alliance. Her territory was not threatened by invasion. To be sure, she could not consider with equanimity the possible repercussions on her national interests of a crushing defeat of France and Belgium. Her position was truly, sincerely, and authoritatively defined by her foreign minister, Sir Edward Grey, when in his famous speech in the House of Commons on August 3, 1914, he deprecated "unconditional neutrality" by declaring:

> If we did take that line by saying, "We will have nothing whatever to do with this matter" under no conditions—the Belgian Treaty obligations, the possible position in the Mediterranean, with damage to British interests, and what may happen to France from our failure to support France—if we were to say that all those things mattered nothing, were as nothing, and to say we would stand aside, we should, I believe, sacrifice our respect and good name and reputation before the world, and should not escape the most serious and grave economic consequences.[15]

It would be most unhistorical and besides unjustly libelous to suspect that British statesmen were determined by other than British interests at the outbreak of the war. But, as soon became obvious, neither the British government, nor the British parliament, nor the British people interpreted British interests in a narrowly nationalistic sense. It was a British interest that international

[15] *Twenty-five Years* (2 vols.; London, 1926), II, 307.

treaties be respected, that international order be not overthrown, that naked force should not triumph over pledged rights, and that the independence of the small free states of Europe be not sacrificed to the territorial ambitions of mighty autocratic empires. As early as August 27, 1914, Mr. Asquith began in his public utterances to stress the general British interest in the maintenance of political freedom on the Continent. On that date he made a speech on Belgium in which he declared:

The war which is now shaking to its foundations the whole European system, originated in a quarrel in which this country had no direct concern. . . . . It is all-important . . . . that it should be clearly understood . . . . why it was that we intervened. . . . . The issue was one which no great and self-respecting nation, certainly none bred and nurtured like ourselves in this ancient home of liberty, could, without undying shame, have declined. . . . . The Belgians have won for themselves the immortal glory which belongs to a people who prefer freedom to ease, to security, to life itself. We are proud of their alliance and their friendship.[16]

Less than a fortnight later, on September 4, 1914, in a recruiting speech at the Guildhall, Mr. Asquith went a step farther in defining the spiritual significance of the great struggle when he declared:

The cynical violation of the neutrality of Belgium was after all but a step, the first step, in a deliberate policy of which, if not the immediate, the ultimate and not far distant aim was

[16] *Speeches by the Earl of Oxford and Asquith*, pp. 202–3.

⟦ 87 ⟧

to crush the independence and the autonomy of the free States of Europe. First Belgium, then Holland and Switzerland—countries like our own imbued and sustained with the spirit of liberty—we were one after the other to be bent to the yoke, and these ambitions were fed and fostered by a body of new doctrines and new philosophy preached by professors and learned men. The free and full self-development which to these small States, to ourselves, to our great and growing Dominions over the seas, to our kinsmen across the Atlantic, is the well-spring and life-breath of national existence; that free self-development is the one capital offence in the code of those who have made force their supreme divinity and upon its altars are prepared to sacrifice both the gathered fruits and potential germs of the unfettered human spirit. I use this language advisedly. This is not merely a material, it is also a spiritual conflict. Upon this issue everything that contains the promise and hope that leads to emancipation and fuller liberty for the millions who make up the masses of mankind will be found sooner or later to depend.[17]

Let us quote one more statement by the British Prime Minister in the second month of the World War. Speaking at Dublin on September 25, 1914, he said:

Forty-four years ago, at the time of the war of 1870, Mr. Gladstone used these words. He said: "The greatest triumph of our time will be the enthronement of the idea of public right as the governing idea of European politics." Nearly fifty years have passed. Little progress, it seems, has as yet been made towards that good and beneficent change, but it seems to me to be now at this moment as good a definition as we can have of our European policy—the idea of public right. What does it mean when translated into concrete terms? It means first and foremost, the clearing of the ground by the definite repudiation of militarism as the

[17] *Ibid.*, pp. 206–7.

governing factor in the relation of States and in the future moulding of the European world. It means next that room must be found and kept for the independent existence and the free development of the smaller nationalities each with a corporate consciousness of its own. Belgium, Holland, and Switzerland, and Scandinavian countries, Greece and the Balkan States—they must be recognized as having exactly as good a title as their more powerful neighbors, more powerful in strength and in wealth, to a place in the sun. And it means finally, or it ought to mean, perhaps by a slow and gradual process, the substitution for force, for the clash of competing ambition, for groupings and alliances and a precarious equipoise, of a real European partnership based on the recognition of equal right and established and enforced by a common will. A year ago that would have sounded like a Utopian idea. It is probably one that may not or will not be realized either to-day or to-morrow. If and when this war is decided in favour of the Allies it will at once come within the range and before long within the grasp of European statesmanship.[18]

In this remarkable and already quite Wilsonian statement, Mr. Asquith not only again stressed the rights of freedom as opposed to the ambitious designs of militaristic violence, but he also, as he complacently remarks in his *Memories and Reflections*, foreshadowed the creation of the League of Nations, that projection of the democratic ideal on the plane of international relations.[19]

In all these public utterances, democracy is, of course, not yet explicitly presented as the common ideal of the Allies, which, in view of the Russian co-operation, would have been tactless no less than

[18] *Ibid.*, p. 218.   [19] Oxford and Asquith, II, 39.

unjustified. But by constantly emphasizing the sympathy of Great Britain with the freedom of the small democratic nations and by opposing this freedom to the threatened domination by militaristic Germany, Mr. Asquith was already very clearly appealing to those sentiments which President Wilson was later to exalt with such telling effect. That such sentiments were shared since the early days of the war in British government circles is shown by a private letter addressed to President Theodore Roosevelt by Sir Edward Grey on December 18, 1914. In this letter Grey, discussing the significance of the war, writes:

> Meanwhile, we have to fight on for three objects:
> (1) To save the British Empire and all that makes life at home here worth living. . . . .
> (2) To get Belgium restored to her people. . . . .
> (3) To secure that the Prussian military party, who prepared and planned this war, shall not in future dominate the policy of Germany.—This, I suppose, can be secured only when the German people realize that they have been deceived and misled by the Yunkers, and whey they turn themselves into a democratic State. It is a difficult thing to arrange, but until it is secured Europe cannot be free from the terrific burden of expenditure on armaments.[20]

The significance of the World War as a struggle for democratic freedom against autocratic militarism was not as early recognized or at least publicly expressed by the political leaders of

[20] *Op. cit.*, II, 142.

France as by their British colleagues. Their reticence may well be accounted for both by the anguish of invasion and by the desire not to alarm their Russian ally. But that this conception was from the start current in France as in England is shown by most of the French war literature. And that it was that of politicians like Briand appears from his speech on November 2, 1915, in the House of Deputies. In that speech, one of the greatest and most effective ever made by that incomparable orator, he asked what peace France would demand once her territory and that of her Belgian and Serbian allies were cleared of invaders. He said:

Shall it be any kind of a peace with which a selfish France, satisfied by the realization of her own national ambitions, could be content? Oh no, Gentlemen! I refuse to believe that my country, which has displayed such magnificent greatness in the circumstances we have been through, should stoop to such a petty and low conception of her role. France in this war—it is her honor and it shall be her glory—is the champion of the whole world.

She stands erect, sword in hand, fighting for civilization and for the independence of the nations. It is only when she will have been guaranteed a lasting, a solid peace, that she will lower her sword. It is only when she and her allies will have bestowed upon the world a peace in which all notions of tyrannical domination will have made way for the idea of civilized progress through the emancipation of the peoples in the free enjoyment of their complete independence.[21]

[21] Quoted from Edgard Milhaud, *La Société des Nations* (Paris, 1917), pp. 63–64.

As the war dragged on, ferociously but inconclusively, the belligerents were beginning to look to the United States with ever greater interest and with alternating hope and anxiety. President Wilson was engaged in the delicate task of defending the neutral rights of his country against the encroachments both of British mastery of the seas and of German submarine warfare. He was attempting to hold the scales well balanced between the rival powers, as well in order to keep America out of the war, as in order to remain for both an acceptable mediator if ever the time for mediation should come.

On December 7, 1915, he delivered his third annual message to Congress. While maintaining what he called a "studiously neutral" attitude, he felt constrained to ask the legislature for increased appropriations for national defense. As a preface to this thankless request and in order to make it more palatable to his audience, he expounded in the following terms his doctrines of democratic peace:

No one who really comprehends the spirit of the great people for whom we are appointed to speak can fail to perceive that their passion is for peace, their genius best displayed in the practice of the arts of peace. Great democracies are not belligerent. They do not seek or desire war. Their thought is of individual liberty and of the free labor that supports life and the uncensored thought that quickens it. Conquest and dominion are not in our reckoning, or agreeable to our principles. But just because we demand unmolested development and the undisturbed government of our own lives upon our own principles of right and liberty, we resent, from whatever quarter it may come, the aggression we ourselves will not practice.[22]

While these remarks were intended primarily for the ears of his own people and of their American neighbors to the south, they could not pass unheeded in Europe, where they of course resounded far more agreeably in London and Paris than in Berlin and Vienna. Commenting on this message in a dispatch addressed to Sir Edward Grey on December 9, 1915, the British Ambassador to Washington wrote:

There is a passage in the President's address to Congress which . . . . very correctly and completely describes the policy of the Allies in Europe in carrying on this war. Those words are applied only to the duties of the United States towards the American continent and the peoples which inhabit it. But no words could better describe the spirit which animates the democracies of Europe at the present time. Gradually, as the struggle goes on, the Kings and the Priests are found as of old, arrayed on one side and the peoples on the other; the war becomes, like many former wars, a struggle for Empire on the one hand and security on the other; more and more the principles of democracy are at stake, and as they are at stake, not only the principles on which this Government is founded but also its political interests and its own security become more and more in danger. This is the feeling which is growing here and it is fair to surmise that it is also in the mind of the President.[23]

[22] *President Wilson's State Papers and Addresses* (New York, 1918), p. 137.

[23] *The Letters and Friendships of Sir Cecil Spring Rice*, II, 303.

More than a year was to pass, however, before the feeling that "the principles of democracy" were at stake in the world was officially expressed by Woodrow Wilson. During that time he had been re-elected to his high office as the chief magistrate who had kept his country out of war. He had continued to maintain an attitude of strict but thwarted neutrality and he had vainly sought to bring the belligerents to the conference table of peace. As late as January 22, 1917, he had, in an address to the American Senate, in reporting on the inconclusive results of his efforts, declared himself in favor of "peace without victory." While this obviously showed that he had then no intention of engaging his country in the conflict, he had added another condition which, in his opinion, the peace he was striving for would have to fulfil in order to be lasting. This other condition he defined and discussed in the following terms:

> No peace can last, or ought to last, which does not recognize and accept the principle that governments derive all their just powers from the consent of the governed. . . . . I speak of this, not because of any desire to exalt an abstract political principle which has always been held very dear by those who have sought to build up liberty in America, but . . . . because I wish frankly to uncover realities. Any peace which does not recognize and accept this principle will inevitably be upset.[24]

[24] *President Wilson's State Papers and Addresses*, p. 353.

This declaration, if it was to be taken at its face value, clearly implied that the universal acceptance of both the doctrines of self-determination and of democracy was in President Wilson's eyes a condition for the establishment of a lasting peace. That it was not everywhere so construed was promptly shown by a German note of January 31, 1917, in which it was said that "the guiding lines of this important declaration agree to a wide extent with the principles and the works which Germany professes."

It was this very note which announced the renewal of unrestricted submarine warfare and thereby led to the abandonment of neutrality by the United States. In announcing the severance of diplomatic relations with Germany on February 3, 1917, President Wilson for the first time and as yet in very cautious terms made the distinction between the "imperial German government" and his "sincere friends . . . . the German people," which was shortly to take such an important place in his foreign policy.[25] All caution and all reticence were thrown to the winds when, finally, on April 2, 1917, President Wilson, addressing Congress, advised that it "declare the recent course of the imperial German government to be in fact nothing less than war against the government and people of the United States." It was from this address

[25] *Ibid.*, p. 362.

that may be dated America's international crusade for democracy, which was to be so successfully pursued until the conclusion of peace. The break with Germany and the recent fall of czarism had obviously released President Wilson from his last inhibitions when, in the course of this address, he made the following statements:

Our object now . . . . is to vindicate the principles of peace and justice in the life of the world as against selfish and autocratic power and to set up amongst the really free and self-governed peoples of the world such a concert of purpose and of action as will henceforth ensure the observance of those principles. . . . . The menace to that peace and freedom lies in the existence of autocratic governments backed by organized force which is controlled wholly by their will, not by the will of their people. . . . . .

We have no quarrel with the German people. We have no feeling towards them but one of sympathy and friendship. It was not upon their impulse that their government acted in entering this war. It was not with their previous knowledge or approval. It was a war determined upon as wars used to be determined upon in the old, unhappy days when peoples were nowhere consulted by their rulers and wars were provoked and waged in the interest of dynasties or of little groups of ambitious men who were accustomed to use their fellow men as pawns and tools. Self-governed nations do not fill their neighbour states with spies or set the course of intrigue to bring about some critical posture of affairs which will give them an opportunity to strike and make conquest. Such designs can be successfully worked out only under cover and where no one has the right to ask questions. . . . . .

Does not every American feel that assurance has been added to our hope for the future peace of the world by the wonderful and heartening things that have been happening within the last few weeks in Russia? Russia was known by those who knew it best to have been always in fact democratic at heart, in all the vital habits of her thought, in all the intimate relationships of her people that spoke their natural instinct, their habitual attitude towards life. The autocracy that crowned the summit of her political structure, long as it had stood and terrible as was the reality of its power, was not in fact Russian in origin, character, or purpose; and now it has been shaken off and the great, generous Russian people have been added in all their naive majesty and might to the forces that are fighting for freedom in the world, for justice, and for peace. . . . .

We are glad, now that we see the facts with no veil of false pretence about them, to fight thus for the ultimate peace of the world and for the liberation of its peoples, the German peoples included: for the rights of nations great and small and the privilege of men everywhere to choose their way of life and of obedience. The world must be made safe for democracy. Its peace must be planted upon the tested foundations of political liberty. . . . .

. . . . right is more precious than peace, and we shall fight for the things which we have always carried nearest our hearts, for democracy, for the right of those who submit to authority to have a voice in their own governments, for the rights and liberties of small nations, for a universal dominion of right by such a concert of free peoples as shall bring peace and safety to all nations and make the world itself at last free. To such a task we can dedicate our lives and our fortunes, everything that we are and everything that we have, with the pride of those who know that the day has come when America is privileged to spend her blood and her might for the principles that gave her birth and happiness and the peace which she has treasured. God helping her, she can do no other.[26]

Commenting on this most extraordinary public utterance by the highest official spokesman of the

[26] *Ibid.*, pp. 378 ff.

potentially most powerful state in the world, Mr. Lloyd George, who was then and remained throughout the peace settlement the British prime minister, is content, in his extremely voluminous *War Memoirs*, to make the following rather ironical remarks:

> These principles were excellent, and excellently expressed. The Allied democracies of France and the British Commonwealth had already borne the burden and been scorched by the heat of a thousand days in the "battle with this natural foe to liberty." They rejoiced at the advent of this powerful help from the greatest democracy in the world, at a time when troubles were multiplying. They perhaps might be excused for thinking that issues so clear now to President Wilson ought to have been apparent earlier to his eyes.[27]

The more detached historian cannot fail to read President Wilson's most astounding pronouncement with far less equanimity. Here was a declaration of war in which the aims defined were no less than the adoption by the enemy of the political philosophy of the new belligerent, and the constitution by the Old World, converted to this philosophy, of a permanent "partnership of democratic nations." What must amaze the historian more still than the audacity of this supremely ambitious program is not that it failed of fulfillment, but rather that it secured such an unusual measure of success.

Two years after it was announced to the world,

[27] III, 1673.

the enemies had not only been obliged to sue for peace but had repudiated their traditional forms of government. Thrones had tottered and been upset all over Europe. New nations, in accordance with the proclaimed doctrine of self-determination, had seen their independence generally recognized and, in accordance with the proclaimed political philosophy, had, as the defeated foes themselves, adopted republican and democratic institutions. And finally the constitution of a permanent League of Nations was being drafted and was shortly to come into force. In the history of international relations there are assuredly few miracles comparable to this. That the miracle wrought by the vision of President Wilson should not have stood the test of time is certainly less surprising than its almost complete, even if only temporary, success itself.

It is not part of our task here to analyze or even to outline the evolution of the Wilsonian philosophy as expounded in his successive public utterances from 1917 to 1919, or its impact on the morale of the belligerents,[28] on the course of their diplomacy, on the downfall of the German and Austro-Hungarian empires, on the negotiations of the armistice, and on the drafting of the treaties

---

[28] It is interesting to note Hitler's infuriated tribute to the efficacy of the Allied war propaganda. Cf. Adolf Hitler, *Mein Kampf* (42d ed.; Munich, 1933), pp. 193 ff. and particularly p. 207.

of peace.[29] Suffice it to recall that the American President, while from time to time adapting his program to the changing exigencies of the military and political situation, remained in all fundamentals true to his general conception as stated in the above-quoted address of April 2, 1917. To the last, the great struggle remained in his eyes a war to establish a lasting peace, based on the universal adoption of national institutions similar to those enjoyed by the United States and guaranteed by and to all democratic peoples. In his Fourteen Points Speech of January 8, 1918, he declared:

What we demand in this war . . . . is that the world be made fit and safe to live in; and particularly that it be made safe for every peace-loving nation which, like our own, wishes to live its own life, determine its own institutions, be assured of justice and fair dealing by the other peoples of the world as against force and selfish aggression.[30]

In his Four Principles Speech of February 11, 1918, he added:

National aspirations must be respected; peoples may now be dominated and governed only by their own consent. "Self-determination" is not a mere phrase. It is an imperative principle of action, which statesmen will henceforth ignore at their peril. . . . . All the parties to this war must join in the settlement of every issue anywhere involved in it; because what we are seeking is a peace that we can all unite to guarantee and maintain. . . . .

[29] These matters have been dealt with in countless publications. Cf. for instance *A History of the Peace Conference of Paris*, ed. H. W. V. Temperley (London, 1920), Vol. I, and my *Uniting Europe* (New Haven, 1930), chap. i.

[30] *President Wilson's State Papers and Addresses*, p. 467.

This war had its roots in the disregard of the rights of small nations and of nationalities which lacked the union and the force to make good their claim to determine their own allegiances and their own forms of political life. Covenants must now be entered into which will render such things impossible for the future; and those covenants must be backed by the united force of all the nations that love justice and are willing to maintain it at any cost. . . . .

Our whole strength will be put into this war of emancipation,—emancipation from the threat and attempted mastery of selfish groups of autocratic rulers.[31]

As all these quotations from President Wilson's war utterances show, his conception was simple, consistent, and fundamentally democratic. Peace cannot be secured unless it be both just in itself and guaranteed by all justice-loving nations. And justice in international affairs means government by the consent of the governed, that is, self-determination and democracy.

In the first volume of the monumental *History of the Peace Conference of Paris* edited by Professor Temperley, of Cambridge, the authors of a study of the historical origins of the general settlement formulated their conclusions in very brief terms. These terms may serve also as a faithful summing-up of our own view of the war as a crusade for democracy. They write:

The President's principles had conquered Europe and the Covenant of Nations remains as the most striking monument to his efforts.

[31] *Ibid.*, pp. 475 ff.

They add somewhat impertinently, writing in 1920: "What still remains to be seen is . . . . whether the Wilsonian principles can conquer America."[32]

Before closing this chapter, we have still to say a word about the democratic repercussions of the World War on the constitutional development of European states. Of such states there were, in 1914, twenty-one, if we disregard the minute principalities and republics of Liechtenstein, Monaco, San Marino, and Andorra. This number was increased by eight and diminished by two as the immediate result of the war. In 1919 there were, therefore, twenty-seven so-called sovereign states in Europe.

Closely to examine the evolution of twenty-seven different constitutions would take more volumes than we can spare pages for this purpose here. How can we, as we therefore obviously must, simplify our task? First of all, we shall leave out of account all the victors and all the neutrals, as well as Bulgaria, which alone of the defeated resembled the former in that she retained her institutions, and Russia, to which we will refer in our next chapter. There remain therefore the five Baltic States—Finland, Lithuania, Esthonia, Latvia, and Poland; the three succession states of

[32] *A History of the Peace Conference of Paris*, I, 204.

Austria-Hungary—Austria, Hungary, and Czechoslovakia; and last, but of course greatest, Germany. Of these, all except the last were in reality
new states which, although they had at one time
or another of their history enjoyed national independence, had lost it long before the beginning
of the World War. It would, therefore, in their
case be more proper to speak of constitutional reconstruction than of constitutional evolution.

However—and that is the second great simpli-
fication of our task—we propose to study neither
the reconstruction nor the evolution of the fundamental laws of any of these nine countries, but
only to note that their peoples were all transferred
by their own free will from the sphere of autocracy
into that of democracy.

Of the five Baltic States, all except Poland, expressly invoking on their behalf the Wilsonian
principle of self-determination, separated themselves from Soviet Russia; Finland at the end of
1917, the three others in 1918. In the course of
the following year they all, by means of popularly
elected diets or constituent assemblies, gave themselves democratic republican constitutions. In
order briefly to show the type of institutions in
which these former subjects of the czar were seeking political happiness, we will be content to quote
a few essential provisions from each of their fundamental laws:

Finland.—Constitution of July 17, 1919:

ARTICLE 1. Finland is a sovereign republic. . . . .

ART. 2. Sovereignty resides in the nation represented in the Diet.

ART. 5. All Finnish citizens are equal before the law.

ART. 17. The organization and the composition of the Diet are defined by the organic law relating to the Diet.

ART. 23. The President of the Republic is elected by the people for six years. He must be a Finnish citizen by birth.[33]

Esthonia.—Constitution of June 15, 1920:

ARTICLE 1. Esthonia is an independent republic in which the sovereign power resides in the people-

ART. 6. All the citizens of the Republic are equal before the law. . . . .

ART. 27. The nation exercises its sovereignty through the citizens enjoying the right of suffrage. This right belongs to all citizens of twenty years of age who have been Esthonians for at least a year.

ART. 29. The people exercise their sovereign rights: (1) by means of the referendum; (2) by means of legislative initiative; (3) by the election of the members of the National Assembly.

ART. 35. The National Assembly exercises legislative powers as representing the people.

ART. 57. The government of the Republic is the executive power in Esthonia.

ART. 58. The government consists of a chief of state and of ministers. . . . .

ART. 59. The National Assembly appoints the government and accepts its resignation.[34]

---

[33] B. Mirkine-Guetzevitch, *Les Constitutions de l'Europe nouvelle* (2d ed.; Paris, 1930), pp. 174 ff. Malbone W. Graham, *New Governments of Eastern Europe* (London, 1928), pp. 169 ff., 621 ff.

[34] Mirkine-Guetzevitch, *op. cit.*, pp. 163 ff., and Graham, *op. cit.*, pp. 246 ff., 646 ff.

〚 104 〛

Latvia.—Constitution of February 15, 1922:

ARTICLE 1. Latvia is an independent democratic republic.

ART. 2. The sovereign power is vested in the people.

ART. 6. The Diet shall be elected by universal, equal, direct and secret vote, on the basis of proportional representation.

ART. 8. Latvian citizens of both sexes, possessing full rights, who shall have attained the age of twenty-one years by the first day of voting, shall have the right to vote.

ART. 35. The President of the state shall be elected by the Diet for a period of three years.

ART. 55. The Cabinet of Ministers shall consist of the Prime Minister and Ministers invited by him.

ART. 56. The Cabinet shall be formed by a person entrusted with that task by the President of the state.

ART. 59. In carrying out their duties, the Prime Minister and Ministers shall of necessity enjoy the confidence of the Diet and shall be responsible to the Diet for their actions. . . . .[35]

Lithuania.—Constitution of August 6, 1922:

SECTION 1. The state of Lithuania is an independent democratic republic.

The sovereign government of the state shall be vested in the people.

SEC. 2. The governmental functions of the state shall be performed by the legislative, the executive and the judicial departments.

SEC. 10. All citizens of Lithuania, men and women, are equal before the law. No special privileges can be given to, nor shall the rights of citizens be restricted because of, race, creed, or nationality.

SEC. 22. The Diet shall be composed of the representatives of the people.

SEC. 23. Representatives shall be elected by a general,

[35] Mirkine-Guetzevitch, *op. cit.,* pp. 235 ff., and Graham, *op. cit.,* pp. 695 ff., 316 ff.

equal, direct and secret ballot based upon a proportional election system. . . . .

Sec. 24. All qualified Lithuanian citizens, men and women, not less than twenty-one years of age, shall have the right to elect representatives to the Diet. . . . .

Sec. 40. The executive authority shall be vested in the President of the Republic and the Cabinet of Ministers.

Sec. 41. The President of the Republic shall be elected by the Diet . . . .

Sec. 47. The President of the Republic shall appoint the Prime Minister, authorize him to form the Cabinet of Ministers, confirm the same, and accept the resignation of the Cabinet of Ministers.

Sec. 59. The Cabinet of Ministers shall be responsible as a whole to the Diet. . . . .

The Ministers must have the confidence of the Diet. If the Diet shall directly declare want of confidence in them, the Cabinet of Ministers and each Minister must resign.[36]

As these brief extracts suffice to show, all these four Baltic countries, as a result of the war, became independent democratic republics. However, their constitutions differed on minor points, their models were clearly American, French, or Swiss. In none is there any trace of Russian influence and in all is the sovereignty vested in the people.

The case of Poland was more interesting still. The problem of devising a constitution adapted to the needs of this new state derived additional complexity from the complexity of its territorial origin. When the war broke out, there had been no independent Poland for nearly one hundred and fifty

[36] Graham, *op. cit.*, pp. 720 ff., 350 ff.

years. Ever since the eighteenth century, the former aristocratic kingdom had remained partitioned between the three autocracies of Russia, Prussia, and Austria. The resurrection of Polish independence cannot be explained merely by the persistence of Polish patriotism in many of the people and especially among their intellectual leaders. It was also due to the fact that these three autocracies, although arrayed in opposite camps at the beginning of the war, were, when it came to an end, all equally defeated and overthrown. When that end came, on October 7, 1918, the Polish Regency Council, which had been set up under Austro-German auspices a year before, issued a manifesto which began thus: "The solemn hour awaited by the nation has just struck. Like the whole world, we adhere to the principles proclaimed by the President of the United States."[37]

The nation to whom these words were addressed was made up of a score of millions of Russian, Austrian, and German subjects, whose ancestors had enjoyed national independence under an aristocratic monarchy and whose most powerful present leader was a former Russian terrorist. That such a nation, in whose historical tradition there was no trace of Western political liberty, should have been led, in 1921, to adopt a republican democratic constitution after the French pat-

[37] *Ibid.*, p. 766.

tern, is assuredly more surprising than the difficulties since encountered in operating it. The constitution of the Republic of Poland adopted on March 17, 1921, by a Constituent Assembly elected in January, 1919, contains the following characteristic provisions:

ARTICLE 1. The Polish state is a republic.

ART. 2. The sovereign power in the Republic of Poland is vested in the nation. This power is exercised through a legislative organ, the Diet and the Senate, through an executive organ, the President of the Republic and responsible Ministers, and through a judicial organ of independent law courts.

ART. 11. The members of the Diet are elected for a period of five years counting from the day of opening of the Diet, by secret, direct and equal vote, on the basis of proportional representation.

ART. 12. The right to vote belongs to all Polish citizens without distinction of sex being twenty-one years of age the day of the summoning of the elections.[38]

The provisions concerning the organization of the executive branch of the government and its relations with the legislature were closely modeled on those of the French constitution. Even before their amendment in 1926, however, the real power belonged to and was exercised by Marshall Pilsudski, whose temperament was always dictatorial and whose socialistic sympathies were never either French or American.

The situation of Czechoslovakia, the first of the

[38] Mirkine-Guetzevitch, *op. cit.*, pp. 256 ff.

three succession states to be considered here, was entirely different.

Although the independence of Bohemia had undergone a still longer historical eclipse than that of Poland, the Czechs, who were the real artisans of its resurrection, were politically and socially, although not racially, far more homogeneous than the Poles. Although the Slovaks had been under Hungarian and the Czechs under Austrian rule, they had long been together subjects of the same emperor-king. Furthermore and much more significant, the Czechs had developed in the relatively liberal pre-war Austrian atmosphere a strong middle-class spirit of nationalism. As the remnants of the local nobility which had survived the suppression of Bohemian independence at the beginning of the seventeenth century were few in number and were co-operating with the Austrian authorities and not opposing them, the way was clear for a truly democratic national resurrection. It is therefore not surprising to find in the Declaration of Independence of the Czechoslovak state issued in Paris on October 18, 1918, over the signatures of Masaryk, Stefanek, and Benes, statements such as the following:

We accept and shall adhere to the ideals of modern democracy, as they have been the ideals of our nation for centuries. We accept the American principles as laid down by President Wilson; the principles of liberated mankind—of the actual equality of nations—and of governments deriving all their just power from the consent of the governed. We, the nation of Comenius, can not but accept these principles expressed in the American Declaration of Independence, the principles of Lincoln, and of the Declaration of the Rights of Man and of the Citizen.[39]

Nor was it surprising that the constitution adopted by the Czechoslovak National Assembly on February 29, 1920, should be that of a completely democratic republic. It most resembled that of France, with its responsible president elected for seven years by the legislature, its Cabinet appointed by the president and holding office as long as assured of a parliamentary majority, and with its House of Deputies and its Senate. The main differences are that in Czechoslovakia both houses are elected directly by the people, who enjoy universal, including female, suffrage, by a system of proportional representation. Furthermore the powers of the Senate are appreciably more restricted than in France and the president has a right of suspensive veto somewhat resembling that of the chief magistrate of the United States.[40]

The political stability shown by Czechoslovakia throughout the first twenty post-war years under most trying external circumstances is not only a tribute to the soundness of its constitution and to

[39] Graham, *New Governments of Central Europe* (London, 1924), pp. 604 ff.

[40] Mirkine-Guetzevitch, *op. cit.*, pp. 324 ff.; Graham, *New Governments of Central Europe*, pp. 268 ff., 602 ff.

the wisdom of its remarkable leaders, it also shows
that here at least the seed of republican democracy,
spread all over the new Europe by President Wilson, fell on a soil well prepared to receive it.

The same can hardly be said of the two other
succession states we are considering here. Pre-war
Hungary was the most oligarchical state of Europe.
Under the crown of the Habsburgs, a powerful,
cultured and wealthy landed aristocracy ruled over
a kingdom in which the Magyars were not even a
majority, but in which the noblemen were but a
very small minority of the Magyars. Of the general
evolution which was carrying Europe from feudalism through royal absolutism or constitutional
monarchy to democracy, they were in reality still
in the first stage.

The Wilsonian doctrine of government by the
consent of the governed was therefore not to be
applied in Hungary without bringing about a complete revolution, social and national as well as
political. Self-determination implied the dismem-
berment of Hungary and republican democracy
the repudiation of all her traditions. The dismem-
berment was achieved to the benefit of all her
neighbors, but the aristocracy refused to repudiate
their traditions and there was no other organized
social group in the state able to take their place.

Thus Hungary, after being in November, 1918,
proclaimed a people's republic by Michael Karolyi,

a Magyar nobleman denounced as a renegade by all his peers, rapidly fell into complete anarchy, a state from which it was not rescued by being declared a soviet republic a few months later. It was only after the soviet dictator Bela Kun had been ousted by foreign intervention that order gradually returned. Today Hungary is a kingdom without a king, in which the traditional aristocracy, which has lost an appreciable part of its property but none of its will to rule, is once more in control of the country.

In Austria, the evolution, while hardly less stormy and less painful, has been very different. Here, also, the Wilsonian propaganda, of which the last foreign minister of the Dual Monarchy says in his war memoirs that it "was a more destructive weapon against us than many army corps,"[41] disrupted the empire and upset the throne of the Habsburgs. But as in the Austrian part of that Empire the prevailing parliamentary constitution had not, as in Hungary, excluded all but a privileged minority from a real participation in public affairs, a basis was found for the establishment of a democratic republic.

As early as November 12, 1918, on the morrow of the withdrawal of Emperor Charles, a first provisional constitution was proclaimed, according

[41] Count J. Andrassy, *Diplomacy and the War* (London, 1921), p. 251.

to the first article of which Austria was declared a "democratic republic." On February 16, 1919, a Constituent Assembly was elected on the broadest possible electoral basis. As a result of the application of the principle of proportional representation, seventy-two Social-Democrats, who were strongly in favor of union with Germany, sixty-nine members of the Christian social party, Catholics who to the last had supported the Habsburgs, and twenty-six representatives of the so-called German parties, were elected. The result of their labors was the so-called "federal constitution" of the Republic of Austria of October 1, 1920, of which the following were some of the most important provisions:

ARTICLE I. Austria is a democratic republic. Sovereignty is vested in the people.

ART. 2. Austria is a federal state. . . . .

ART. 7. All citizens are equal before the law. No privilege may be established based either on birth, sex, condition, class or confession.

ART. 24. The legislative function is exercised conjointly by the National Council elected by the whole nation and the Federal Council elected by the provincial diets.

ART. 26. The National Council is elected by the whole nation on the basis of equal, direct, secret and personal suffrage. All men and all women who shall be twenty years of age in the year of the elections may vote.

ART. 38. The National Council and the Federal Council meet in public session as Federal Assembly at the seat of the former to elect the President of the Confederation.

ART. 60. (1). The President of the Confederation is elected by the Federal Assembly by secret ballot.

(2). His term of office is four years. He may be immediately reëlected only once.

ART. 69. (1). The supreme functions of the federal administration, except those of the President of the Confederation, are entrusted to the Federal Chancellor, to the Vice-Chancellor and to the other federal Ministers. Together they constitute the federal Government under the chairmanship of the Chancellor. . . . .

ART. 70. The federal Government is elected by roll call by the National Council.[42]

These articles, especially when considered together with the rather complicated provisions concerning the legislative initiative and referendum, suffice to show that the Austrian federal constitution most resembled those of Switzerland and of the United States.

However important the adoption of democratic institutions in all the states we have mentioned heretofore, it was the forced conversion of the German Empire to the Wilsonian ideals that constituted the most significant triumph of the latter in Europe.

As is well remembered, it was only under the triple pressure of military defeat, of starvation, and of Wilsonian diplomacy that, in the autumn of 1918, Germany abandoned her monarchical institutions. Her retreat was gradual, but it ended in a rout.

Toward the end of August, 1918, Prince Max of

[42] Mirkine-Guetzevitch, pp. 126 ff.; Graham, *New Governments of Central Europe*, pp. 131 ff., 501 ff.

Baden, who was a liberal constitutionalist but still an opponent of government by parliament, offered his services as chancellor to Emperor William II, in the hope of promoting peace and of saving the monarchical tradition. On September 29 this offer, which had been declined on September 11, was accepted. On October 9 the first note of the State Department was received in Berlin. To the query it contained as to who was in effect responsible for Germany's policy, Prince Max could, on October 14, truthfully reply that his government enjoyed the confidence of the Reichstag, which had been elected on the basis of manhood suffrage. Wilson's third note, of October 23, with its final allusion to "military rulers and monarchical autocrats" led to the adoption on October 28 of a constitutional amendment establishing the principle of parliamentary responsibility. On November 9 Prince Max, announcing that the Emperor had decided to renounce the throne, turned over the chancellorship to the socialist Ebert.[43]

On January 19, 1919, a National Constituent Assembly was elected by over thirty million German male and female citizens voting freely and secretly. On July 31, 1919, the Weimar Constitution, in essentials the work of Dr. Hugo Preuss,

[43] Graham, *New Governments of Central Europe*, pp. 16 ff., and Rappard, *Uniting Europe* (New Haven, 1930), pp. 16 ff.

a constitutional lawyer of Jewish blood and a member of the democratic party, was adopted by a majority of three hundred sixty-two votes against seventy-five. Although it was not submitted to a popular vote, there is no reason to believe that it did not at the time satisfy the majority of the German people.

The Weimar Constitution is too well known to call for any analysis here. Suffice it to say that by this fundamental law the German people were placed in complete and unfettered control of their national destinies. In all its provisions it is a faithful implementation of the principles of republican democracy affirmed in its first article, which reads: "The Reich is a republic. All political authority is derived from the people."

With the conversion of the German people to these principles so utterly contrary to their national traditions, it seemed as if the European world had truly been made safe for democracy. An American president, although no longer the hero of his own people, had in fact become the supreme lawgiver of Europe, and the law he gave Europe was the law of democracy, which had apparently gained more ground in Europe in the course of a few months than it had won in as many centuries before.

CHAPTER IV

THE RISE OF POST-WAR
DICTATORSHIPS

We have seen in the preceding chapter that at the end of the World War the talk was everywhere of the triumph of democracy, not of its crisis. But already in 1927 a former prime minister of Italy could write:

In any case, the result of the war has been that two great European States have lost their freedom, and others are in danger of losing it.

Russia and Italy are now in fact ruled by minority Governments, with conflicting aims, yet both based upon force.

Besides this there are dictatorships of varying types, or reactionary Governments, in Spain, Turkey, Poland, Portugal, Hungary, Rumania, Bulgaria, and Greece.

Hardly one of the Austro-Hungarian Succession States has retained its freedom. At any rate, that is true of the large populations representing other nationalities. . . . .

In Great Britain, France, Belgium, Holland, and the Scandinavian countries, and even in Germany, it seems that democracy and the development of free institutions have nothing to fear and are definitely assured.

But even in countries where democracy has long been established reactionary parties are not lacking; they aim at the forcible seizure of power by minorities, and at more or less camouflaged dictatorship.[1]

[1] Francesco Nitti, *Bolshevism, Fascism and Democracy* (London, 1927), pp. 16–17.

THE CRISIS OF DEMOCRACY

Today the position of democracy in the world seems even more critical than it did ten years ago. Not only has the circle of dictatorships been extended to include practically the whole of central, eastern, and southern Europe, but also in Spain, the one antidictatorial movement which in the meanwhile had been momentarily successful is at the moment of writing again succumbing to the renewed assaults of internal and external foes of democracy. Everywhere the friends of political liberty and of popular government are on the defensive today, and the League of Nations, which was clearly the child of their hopes and of their efforts, is crippled and paralyzed.

What has happened in the course of the last twenty years to explain this historical revulsion, as sudden as it is extensive in its incidence?

Before inquiring into the causes and conditions of this disease, if, as we believe, it be a disease, that is, a morbid state of human society, let us examine its principal symptoms. These symptoms we find in the collapse of liberal regimes and the rise of dictatorships, on the one hand, and, on the other, in the difficulties encountered in the normal working of free institutions in the surviving democracies. In this chapter we propose to deal with the first of these symptoms. In the following we shall consider the second. In speculating on the future of democracy in our final chapter, we shall revert to the causes and conditions which may help to explain its present crisis.

The first in date of the post-war dictatorships was that which emerged from the Russian Revolution of 1917. It sought to establish what, in accordance with pre-war Marxism, it called the dictatorship of the proletariat, but what, in fact, resulted in the suppression of all public liberty in favor of one autocratic ruler. This dictatorship was not only chronologically the first, it was perhaps also the first in importance, since it has established its domination over the largest country of Europe, since it professes world-wide ambitions, and since it has supplied the justification, or at least a partial pretext, for most of the others.

In the few pages at our disposal for the purpose, we can do no more than to recall briefly the main phases of the Russian Revolution of 1917 and to examine its historical significance in the light of the assertions of its principal actors.

If we compare the march of the Russian Revolution with that of the popular movements which, two years later, led to the overthrow of existing autocracies and to the adoption of democratic constitutions, we cannot fail to be struck by certain superficial analogies in the succession of external events during its first two stages.

As a general background: military defeat, economic misery of the masses, lost confidence in the leaders, hope for a prompter cessation of hostilities and for more favorable peace terms.[2]

First act: the autocratic ruler, faced with the undisguised hostility of his civilian subjects, turns to the army. He is disappointed with his reception. After many hesitations, having consulted with his senior generals and having received more and more urgent suggestions from his political advisers, he finally decides to abdicate, as a rule too late thereby to stop the revolution.

Czar Nicholas II abdicated on March 15, 1917, in favor of his brother the Grand Duke Michael, who immediately felt obliged to follow suit.[3]

Second act: a provisional government is formed, in which the reins of power are taken over by the more moderate elements of the malcontents in the hope that by amnesties, promises of the summoning of a constituent assembly, and other concessions, the revolutionaries will be appeased.

On the very day of the czar's abdication a provisional government was formed by an unofficial committee of the Duma, which had itself recently adjourned. The provisional government was com-

[2] Paul Miliukov, *Russlands Zusammenbruch* (2 vols.; Berlin, 1925), I, 17 ff.; Alexander F. Kerensky, *The Catastrophe* (New York, 1927), pp. 1 ff.; Leon Trotsky, *The History of the Russian Revolution*, trans. from the Russian (3 vols.; London, 1932–34), I, 36 ff.

[3] Kerensky, *op. cit.*, pp. 45 ff.; Trotsky, *op. cit.*, I, 106 ff.

posed of liberal and progressive members of the Duma. Its president was Prince Lvov, and its first real leader the Foreign Minister Paul Miliu- kow, a historian and a member of the liberal Cadet party. The only representative of the workers in the new ministry was Alexander Kerensky, a moderate socialist lawyer who had been elected vice-president of the Petrograd Soviet. As he re- lates himself, the executive committee had de- cided "that the representatives of the revolu- tionary democracy 'could not take office in the Provisional Government because the government and the whole Revolution were bourgeois.'" He therefore felt confronted by what he called "a painful question, having to choose between leav- ing the Soviet and remaining in the government or remaining in the Soviet and refusing to take part in the government. Both alternatives seemed im- possible to me," he added.[4]

According to Trotsky, who was still in America at the time and who in his *History* of course shows little patience with this future enemy of the Bol- sheviks, this is how Kerensky answered his "pain- ful question":

. . . . he appeared at a plenary session of the Soviet . . . . requested the floor for a special announcement, and in a speech . . . . demanded the personal confidence of the deputies, and spoke of his general readiness to die for the revolution, and his

[4] *Op. cit.*, p. 53.

more immediate readiness to take the portfolio of Minister of Justice. . . . . There was no vote. Kerensky decided to interpret the applause as a vote of confidence. In a way he was right. The Soviet was undoubtedly in favour of socialists entering the ministry, seeing in that a step toward the liquidation of the bourgeois government with which it had not for a moment reconciled itself.[5]

From the start, this provisional government, which therefore represented an imaginary middle-class democracy, which owed its official position to forces beyond its control, and which pledged itself to the continuance of an almost universally unpopular war, enjoyed little moral and hardly more coervice authority. It was comparable to the helmsman of a dismantled ship driving before a gale. Describing its impotence, Trotsky quotes a contemporary reactionary wit who "characterized the situation thus: 'The old government is in prison, and the new one under house arrest.' "[6]

One of the first official acts of the provisional government was the publication on March 17, 1917, of an appeal to the nation. This brief document, which contained no specific allusion either to the circumstances which led to the defeat of what are merely referred to as "the noxious forces of the old regime," or to the foreign policy of the new government, declares the government to be composed of "men whose past political and public activity assures them the confidence of the country."

[5] *Op. cit.*, I, 201.   [6] *Ibid.*, p. 215.

Besides promising a series of concessions and reforms, its authors state that they intend to make
"immediate preparations for the summoning of a
constituent assembly, which, with universal suffrage as a basis, shall establish the governmental
regime and the constitution of the country."[7]

So far, the Russian Revolution of March, 1917,
closely resembles, in what may be termed revolutionary procedure, that which two or three years
later led to the establishment of democratic institutions in all the other countries mentioned in our
last chapter. It is in the third and final act only
that the Russian drama becomes truly original.
Before the unduly delayed meeting of the Constituent Assembly, there appeared on the scene a new
body of leaders for whom democracy was not
enough.

On the third of April, writes Trotsky, "Lenin
arrived in Petrograd from abroad. Only from that
moment does the Bolshevik Party begin to speak
out loud, and, what is more important, with its
own voice."[8]

Lenin, who for years had been rehearsing in
Switzerland his chosen part as the real leader of a
world-revolution which he hoped to see and to accomplish, was in the first months of 1917 "raging

[7] M. W. Graham, *New Governments of Eastern Europe* (London,
1928), p. 568.

[8] *Op. cit.*, I, 298.

in his Zurich cage seeking a way out." That way out was at last kindly shown to him by the German general staff, for whom he was, to be sure, a strange bedfellow, but still a not unwelcome ally.

What Lenin's conception of the Russian Revolution was when he left Switzerland, we know from his "Farewell Letter to the Swiss Workers" of April 8, 1917. In this letter, we read:

> To the Russian proletariat has fallen the great honour of *initiating* the series of revolutions which are arising from the imperialist war with objective inevitability. But the idea that the Russian proletariat is a chosen revolutionary proletariat among the workers of the world is absolutely alien to us. We know full well that the proletariat of Russia is *less* organised, less prepared, and less class conscious than the proletariat of other countries. It is not any particular virtues it possessed, but rather the specific historical circumstances, that have made the proletariat of Russia for a certain, *perhaps very brief,* period the skirmishers of the world revolutionary proletariat.
>
> Russia is a peasant country, one of the most backward of European countries. Socialism *cannot triumph there directly at once.* But the peasant character of the country, coupled with the vast land possessions of the noble landlords, *may,* to judge by the experience of 1905, give tremendous scope to the bourgeois-democratic revolution in Russia, and make our revolution a *prelude* to and a *step* towards the world socialist revolution.[9]

On arriving in Russia, Lenin at once advocated a policy opposed not only to that of the provisional government but also to that of the Soviets which were springing up all over the country and of which

[9] V. I. Lenin, *Selected Works* (London, 1936), VI, 17.

the Petrograd unit, which had elected Kerensky, was the most important.

He stated on April 20, 1917:

> The fact must be recognized that in most of the Soviets of Workers' Deputies our Party is in a minority, and so far in a small minority, as against *a bloc of all* the petty-bourgeois opportunist elements, who have yielded to the influence of the bourgeoisie and are the conveyors of its influence to the proletariat.[10]

Two days later he wrote:

> . . . . side by side with the Provisional Government, the government of the *bourgeoisie*, there has developed *another* government, weak and embryonic as yet, but undoubtedly an actually existing and growing government—the Soviet of Workers' and Soldiers' Deputies.
>
> What is the class composition of this other government? It consists of the proletariat and the peasantry (clad in army uniform). What is the political nature of this government? It is a revolutionary dictatorship, i.e., a power based on outright revolutionary seizure, on the direct initiative of the masses from below, and not on a *law* made by a centralised government. It is an entirely different power from that of the ordinary type of parliamentary bourgeois-democratic republic which has hitherto prevailed in the advanced countries of Europe and America.[11]

These quotations suffice to show why the ambitions of the Communist party, as set forth by its leader, who was soon to become its dictator, were incompatible not only with the maintenance of the provisional government but also with the estab-

[10] *Ibid.*, VI, 22.

[11] *Ibid.*, p. 27.

lishment of a democratic constitution. The events of the next six months were to show it more clearly still.

After several successive changes in the personnel of the provisional government, from which Miliukow resigned and of which Kerensky became the effective head in May; after bloody uprisings of the Communists in July, in the course of which Lenin was obliged to flee, and Trotsky, who had arrived from America, was arrested; after the armed intervention of General Korniloff who, instead of supporting the government, turned against it, the Bolsheviks finally succeeded in gaining control in November, 1917, by a coup d'état. As Kerensky wrote: "The struggle of the organized forces of democracy ended in complete failure, under the pressure of the supporters of dictatorship on the Right and the Left."[12]

The Constituent Assembly was finally elected a fortnight later. This is how Trotsky referred to the event which ever since the Revolution of 1905 had been proclaimed by the enemies of czarism as the goal of their efforts and the instrument of their liberation:

Not one party had yet withdrawn the slogan of the Constituent Assembly, and this included the Bolsheviks. But almost unnoticeably in the course of the events of the revolution, this chief democratic slogan, which had for a decade and

[12] *Op. cit.*, p. 372.

a half tinged with its colour the heroic struggle of the masses, had grown pale and faded out, had somehow been ground between millstones, had become an empty shell, a form naked of content, a tradition and not a prospect. There was nothing mysterious in this process. The development of the revolution had reached the point of a direct battle for power between the two basic classes of society, the bourgeoisie and the proletariat. A Constituent Assembly could give nothing either to the one or the other. The petty bourgeoisie of the town and country could play only an auxiliary and secondary rôle in this conflict. They were in any case incapable of seizing the power themselves. If the preceding months had proved anything, they had proved that. Nevertheless in a Constituent Assembly the petty bourgeoisie might still win—and they actually did win as it turned out—a majority. And to what end? Only to the end of not knowing what to do with it. This reveals the bankruptcy of formal democracy in a deep historic crisis.[13]

Although the Bolsheviks, being in power, naturally hoped that the elections would bring them a majority, they were to be disappointed. According to Lenin's own figures, they polled no more than 25 per cent of a total vote of over thirty-six millions, the absolute majority being won by the more moderate Socialists and peasants who had supported Kerensky[14] and who refused to give their approval to its overthrow.

Lenin, however, did not dream of bowing to the will of the majority, and when the Constituent Assembly met for its first session on January 18,

[13] *Op. cit.*, III, 87–88.

[14] *Op. cit.*, VI, 464.

1918, it was dispersed, writes Kerensky, by the vehemence of drunken bolshevist sailors.[15]

Lenin justified his action in an article entitled "The Elections to the Constituent Assembly and the Dictatorship of the Proletariat," which he published in December, 1919. He wrote:

How then could such a miracle as the victory of the Bolsheviks have occurred, when the Bolsheviks received only one-quarter of the votes. . . . . For it would be simply ridiculous to deny the victory now, when the Entente—the almighty Entente—has for two years been lending aid to every enemy of the Bolsheviks. . . . .

The Bolsheviks triumphed primarily because they had the support of the overwhelming majority of the proletariat, among them the most class conscious, energetic and revolutionary section, the true vanguard of this advanced class.

Let us take the two capitals, Petrograd and Moscow. In these two cities a total of 1,765,100 votes were cast in the elections to the Constituent Assembly, of which the Socialist-Revolutionaries polled 218,000, the Bolsheviks 837,000, and the Cadets 515,400.

Notwithstanding the ardent genuflections of the petty-bourgeois democrats who call themselves Socialists and Social-Democrats (the Chernovs, Martovs, Kautskys, Longuets, MacDonalds and Co.) before the altar of the goddesses of "equality," "universal suffrage," "democracy," "pure democracy" and "consistent democracy," the economic and political fact of the *inequality* of town and country cannot be effaced.

It is a fact inevitable under capitalism in general, and in the transition from capitalism to communism in particular.

Under the conditions of the present historical era, the town cannot be the equal of the country and the country cannot be the equal of the town. The town will inevitably *lead* the

[15] *Op. cit.*, p. 374.

country. The country will inevitably *follow the town.* The only question is, *which class* of the "town classes" will succeed in leading the country, will achieve this aim, and what forms this *leadership of the town* will take.[16]

The leadership of the urban population in such an agricultural country as Russia is clearly the dictatorship of the minority. That the Russian Communists were and are a minority, and that this government is therefore dictatorial is not only their admission but their boast. They recall that Karl Marx, in criticizing the Socialist program adopted at Gotha in 1875, had written:

Capitalist and communist society are separated by a period of revolutionary change from one into the other. To this period corresponds a political period of transition in which the state can be no other than the revolutionary dictatorship of the proletariat.[17]

What interests us here, however, more than the historical origin of the term, is the emergence of the fact. It has recently been attributed to the circumstance that Lenin

combined in himself two traditions: the tradition of the Russian revolutionary intelligentsia in its most maximalist tendency, and the tradition of Russian Government in its most despotic aspect.[18]

[16] *Op. cit.,* VI, 466–67.

[17] Quoted by T. G. Masaryk, *Les Problèmes de la démocratie* (Paris, 1924), p. 111.

[18] Nicholas Berdyaev, *The Origin of Russian Communism,* trans. from the Russian (London, 1937), p. 143.

The despotic aspect of the Bolshevik dictatorship today more and more completely eclipses the
Communist aspect. It is not only the dictatorship
of the urban proletariat over the whole country,
nor is it even only the dictatorship of the Communist vanguard over the proletariat, which is
endlessly expounded, interpreted, and justified by
Stalin, who places himself under the authority of
Lenin, as Lenin invoked that of Karl Marx.[19] It
has today become the dictatorship of a man over
the Communist vanguard itself.

In 1927 Stalin explained to the first American
labor delegation in Russia that Lenin had taken
over from Marx and Engels "the fundamental idea
of the dictatorship of the proletariat as the political
domination of the proletariat and as a method of
overthrowing the reign of capital by violence." He
added that among Lenin's personal contributions
to the doctrine was the particular emphasis he laid
upon the

fact that the dictatorship of the proletariat is a higher type
of democracy in class society, the form of *proletarian* democracy, expressing the interests of the majority (the exploited),
as against capitalist democracy, which expresses the interests
of the minority (the exploiters).[20]

By this learned exegesis of the scripture of communism and of its interpretation by the father of

[19] Joseph Stalin, *Leninism*, trans. from the Russian (2 vols.;
London, 1928-33), I, 20 ff., 110 ff., 161 ff.

[20] *Op. cit.*, II, 44.

bolshevism, Mr. Stalin may have impressed, mystified, and perhaps even convinced some of his American listeners. But he could hardly thereby have justified his own policy, by virtue of which it is not only a class that rules over a nation, or a party over a class, or the party leaders over the party, but finally also a party dictator over the party leaders.

If this is proletarian democracy, does it not strangely resemble that other form of autocracy which for centuries has disgraced czarism in the eyes of the world? Has it not inherited both the unparliamentary absolutism and the cruelly ruthless police methods of the latter? If the dictatorship of the proletariat, which was intended to free the multitudes of the exploited, in fact resolves itself into the undisputed dictatorship of a single leader, no wonder that it has come to be looked upon with ever greater suspicions by the free countries of the world.

The circumstances which led to the establishment of the bolshevist dictatorship in Russia are, however, much easier to understand than the claims of the present dictator to the title of chief emancipator of the workers of the world. Undoubtedly there is a logical connection between the theoretical dictatorship of the proletariat as a program of action and the effective dictatorship of an individual as the practical outcome. When once a popular movement, having from the start repudiated both metaphysics and tradition as a guiding principle, also abandons the solid ground of democracy, it can found its authority only on superior insight which, in the absence of any free and impartial judge, means superior force. The leader of such a movement, even if we suppose him to be devoid of all personal ambition and devoted solely to the interests of his followers, who are no longer his constituents, will naturally see in the liberty of all possible rivals an obstacle to his own ascendancy and to the common good. That is why after the downfall of czarism and the suppression of democracy, the freedom of the Russian proletariat, the rights of its reputed vanguard, the Communist party, and finally even the life of all its most ancient, most faithful, and most influential servants and leaders have all come to be sacrificed to the overpowering will of one supreme individual.

The dictatorship of the proletariat in Russia, which has resolved itself into the dictatorship of comrade Stalin was clearly the child of national defeat. A small band of revolutionaries, many of whom had lived in exile abroad and among whom the Jews were always numerous, had for years been conspiring against the czarist regime. When they saw their country staggering under the blows of a foreign invader, they felt that their day had come. With the help of the invader and by promises of immediate peace on his own terms, they obtained the necessary backing among revolted urban laborers and mutinous soldiers to impose their will on the enfeebled and disunited majority of the national community.

The origins of the second dictatorship to gain control of one of the great powers of Europe were very different. As Russian bolshevism had been born of national defeat, Italian fascism was the offspring of disappointed national victory. As the Russian Bolshevists had made stock of the war weariness of the crushed Russian people, the Italian Fascists appealed to the injured pride of their youth, to whom victory had brought more disillusionment than satisfaction. As the Russian Bolshevists achieved their aims, which were professedly social, at the expense of the national interest, the Italian Fascists achieved theirs, which were outspokenly nationalistic, at the expense of those of their compatriots whose concern was more with the maintenance of internal liberty than with national aggrandizement.

It should be noted, on the other hand, that both movements, however dissimilar their origins and their spirit, were the direct outcome of the World War and owed their triumph to the war-caused social dislocation and demoralization which had weakened the resistance of their opponents. It should be noted, furthermore, that although neither of these movements at the outset was professedly aimed at the suppression of political liberty and at the establishment of an individual dictatorship, such have been the results achieved by both. And today democracy is being derided and denounced in Rome at least as insistently and as vociferously as in Moscow.

The task of the foreign student for whom Italian fascism holds no more allurement than Russian bolshevism, but who wishes to consider them with equal fairness, is assuredly not an easy one. Bolshevism, in spite of its industrial achievements, has, by persecuting and executing the great majority of its own leaders for political reasons, in a way refuted itself as a scheme of government. Not so fascism. However repugnant its internal policies must be to all lovers of liberty, and however abhorrent its foreign policies to all friends of peace and international order, it must be admitted that it has not only maintained itself, its leader, and its party, but that, judged by its own standards, it has been uncommonly successful in many fields.

But how real, how lasting, and how significant are its achievements in the fields, for instance, of economic equipment, social organization, church policy, diplomacy, and war? What of the state and degree of prosperity of the country or the state and degree of contentment of its people? All these are questions about which one hears the most contradictory opinions. These opinions are indeed so consistently conflicting according to the political sympathies of those who profess them both within and without Italy, that they would seem to offer a surer clue to these sympathies than to the real situation.

These uncertainties are mentioned here only to emphasize the difficulty confronting the impartial observer who wishes not to judge the regime in the light of his own general philosophy but to know and to understand the facts concerning its advent.

Of these facts one, at least, is above all discussion. The political situation of Italy from the time of the armistice in 1918 until the march on Rome, in October, 1922, was most unsatisfactory for everyone. Whether we examine it as it is described by politicians such as Signor Mussolini himself,[21] or by his bitterest enemies such as Signor Nitti[22] or Don Sturzo,[23] or whether we consult the writings of historians of pro- or anti-Fascist leanings such as Luigi Villari,[24] on the one hand, and

[21] Benito Mussolini, *My Autobiography* (New York, 1928), pp. 59 ff.; *Edition définitive des œuvres et discours*, French trans. (10 vols.; Paris), Vol. III.

[22] *Op. cit.*, pp. 42 ff.

[23] *Italy and Fascismo* (London, 1926), pp. 42 ff.

[24] *Italy* (London, 1929), pp. 147 ff.

Silvio Trentin,[25] Egidio Reale,[26] and H. Finer,[27] on the other, the picture is, if not the same, at least equally distressing.

A discredited parliament which had not willed the war, which for fear of dangerous controversy had seldom met during its course, and which, during its aftermath, devised no constructive policies, supported no reliable government, but overthrew five almost equally weak cabinets in the space of four years; fluctuating and unsuccessful foreign policies, which disappointed the hopes of the victorious Italian people and lessened the prestige of their country abroad; feeble financial policies which, in spite of increasing taxation, led to excessive indebtedness and to monetary inflation; a disillusioned, disgruntled, revolted people, who displayed their contempt for all authority, occupying factories and multiplying strikes even in the essential public services.

If such was democracy—a "worn-out democracy," in Mussolini's words[28]—and such its fruits, it is no wonder that the daring of its enemies was sooner or later to overcome the resistance of its champions. But that in spite of universal suffrage and unlimited individual freedom Italian

[25] *Antidémocratie* (Paris, 1930), pp. 7 ff.

[26] *L'Aventure italienne* (Paris, 1938), pp. 17 ff.; *L'Italie* (Paris, 1934), pp. 31 ff.

[27] *Mussolini's Italy* (London, 1935).   [28] *My Autobiography*, p. 88.

parliamentarism, with what Don Sturzo calls its "disguised dictatorships"[29] of heads of rival political coteries, could truly be called democracy, is at least doubtful. Parliament was the legal organ for the expression of the popular will. As all recognized, however, that will never succeeded in finding faithful parliamentary expression.

On November 11, 1918, a former Socialist, who had urged his country to enter the war and had fought and bled in the trenches, made an open-air speech in Milan to celebrate the victory. In the course of his oration, he declared:

Do you recall last year at this same date? Do you recall how last year we swore that the Huns would not cross the Piave? They did not cross it. . . . . We then saw the first Poilu, the first "Tommies": it was the Entente which had come to cement the alliance in our trenches. After a year of sacrifice and of faith, here is victory. . . . . We have today realized our ideals. We have attained our national aims: the Italian flag floats today from the Brenner to Trieste, over Fiume, over Zara, those most Italian of cities. . . . . We have also attained the international aims of our War. When we said to you four years ago that the red flag would wave over the castle of Potsdam, the dream seemed a folly. Today the Kaiser is running away and militarism disappearing with the Hohenzollerns. The most extraordinary political panorama is unfolding itself before an astonished universe. Empires, kingdoms, autocracies are tumbling as a house of cards. Austria is no more: imperial Germany in its turn will disappear tomorrow. At the cost of our blood, we have given the German people its freedom, while the German people were shedding their blood to throw us into the chains of imperialism

[29] *Op. cit.*, p. 67.

and military slavery. The ideal dream of the League of Nations begins to come true on the ruins of the old world.

Victory must now bring us its prize also within our frontiers: the redemption of the workers. The Italian people must in future be the arbiters of their own destiny. The workers must be freed from the shackles of speculation and of misery. . . . . Today Italy is no longer a slave; she is mistress of herself and of her destiny. She is no longer a ship without a helmsman in a storm, since a magnificent horizon is opening up before her with victory. The whole Italian people is at the helm of the ship which, majestically riding the waves between three seas and three continents, is serenely and securely proceeding towards the haven of supreme justice, the haven of emancipated mankind of tomorrow.[30]

This confident and optimistic orator, this passionate foe of the Huns, of imperial thrones and autocratic militarism, this grateful friend of France and of Great Britain, this enthusiastic supporter of the League of Nations, this contented Italian patriot, this liberal emancipator of the working classes, was Benito Mussolini.

This son of a blacksmith of the Romagna, a "sulphurous land" of the northeast of Italy, as he called it, was then thirty-five years of age. He had begun life as a primary-school teacher and had then, for a short time, earned a meager living as a mason in Switzerland, attending university courses of economics under Pareto in Lausanne in his spare hours. His extremist revolutionary views which he expounded before labor meetings led to his expulsion first from two Swiss cantons. For an

[30] Œuvres et discours, I, 360–61.

incendiary article he was then expelled from Austria, where he had followed his friend the journalist Cesare Battisti whose "aspirations as a socialist patriot," as Mussolini calls him, appealed to him. In 1912, at the age of twenty-nine, he became chief editor of the "Avanti," the organ of the Italian Socialist party, in which he represented the revolutionary wing. He had already, as he states in his *Autobiography*, "understood . . . . that the Gordian knot of Italian political life could only be undone by an act of violence."[31]

When the war came, he broke with his paper and his party because he refused to be associated with the policy of neutrality they had officially adopted. Instead he "created the Fascisti—a group of daring youths who believed that intervention could be forced." He was bitterly opposed to the Liberal Democratic pacifist group headed by Giolitti who, as he writes, "was busy in the attempt to find a formula which would solve the problem of righting the borders of Italy, but which would save our country from the burden, the sacrifice and the loss of life that every war imposes."[32]

He considered this "weak statesmanship—the statesmanship of compromise," and he adds, in his *Autobiography*:

There were seers who saw in the European conflict not only national advantages but the possibility of a supremacy

[31] *Autobiography*, p. 18.   [32] *Ibid.*, p. 37.

of race. In the cycle of time, again a dramatic period had come which was making it possible for Italy by the weight of its army to deal as an equal with the leading nations of the world.

That was our chance. I wanted to seize it. It became my one thought of intensity.[33]

On November 15, 1914, Mussolini published the first number of the *Popolo d'Italia*, the paper which has ever since been, with his own popular eloquence, his principal weapon in all the political struggles in which he has been engaged.

After the delivery of the exultant and optimistic speech which he had made in Milan on the morrow of victory, his first important political act was the foundation on March 23, 1919, of the Fascist party. Referring to this event in his *Autobiography*, published eight years later, he writes: "I speak of movement and not of party, because my conception always was that Fascism must assume the characteristics of being anti-party."[34]

However, as it was given a program, as it was founded with a view to a legislative election, for which it set up its own candidates, it is impossible to deny that even if it was not merely a political party it was a real party. This is so obvious that Mussolini himself, speaking, a few pages later in his *Autobiography*, of the elections of 1919, recognizes it by writing: "I wanted the Fascisti to try

[33] P. 38.   [34] P. 68.

alone the chance of the elections. We did not ally ourselves with any other party."[35]

The first program of the Fascists is, however, much more interesting to us than their definition. It shows that, movement or party, they were essentially a war product, proud of having taken part in it, proud of having brought their country into it, proud of its results for Italy and also for the whole world. A few quotations will illustrate this more clearly, more convincingly, and more concisely than any comment. We read in this program:

> This war we have willed it: it was not imposed upon us; we could have avoided it. If we took this course it means that there are in our past, in our blood, elements and so to speak ferments of greatness.[36]

Toward the end of the program, Mussolini, for he was really its author, adds the following characteristic statement:

> I feel no enthusiasm for battles fought with voting ballots, as I have shown long ago by suppressing all reviews of parliamentary debates in my paper. . . . . But this year there are to be elections . . . . in which our participation in the war will be attacked. . . . . We accept the challenge particularly on this issue. Not only are we not sorry for what we have done, but we go further: with the courage which is the fruit of our individualism, we declare that if, in Italy, the situation again became what it was in 1915, we would again demand to make war as we did in 1915.[37]

[35] P. 81.

[36] Mussolini, *Œuvres et discours*, I, 371. [37] *Ibid.*, p. 373.

This Fascist pride in the war was, of course, primarily national, the joy of national aggrandizement. But that in March, 1919, that is, before the disappointments of the peace settlement, it was still also more than national, is shown by the following quotations:

> The meeting of March 23 declares that it combats the imperialism of other peoples at the expense of Italy and Italian imperialism at the expense of other peoples should such ever arise. It accepts the supreme principle of the League of Nations which consecrates in advance the integrity of each of its members.

However, on imperialism and the League of Nations, the doctrine of Mussolini was already apprehensively critical, as he added to the foregoing statement the declaration:

> Imperialism is the vital spring of every people which tends to economic and moral aggrandizement. What distinguishes the various forms of imperialism are the means employed for the attainment of their ends. Those which we may and shall choose will never be the methods of barbarous penetration adopted by the Germans and we say: either all idealists or none. Let everyone follow his own interests. One would not understand that those who are in comfortable circumstances should present idealism to those who suffer, that would be too easy. We want our place in the world because we have a right to it. I again here, in this order of the day, approve the doctrine of the League of Nations. This doctrine is ours after all, but let there be no misunderstanding: if the League of Nations is to be nothing but a solemn trick to be played by the wealthy nations on the proletarian nations for the establishment and for the perpetuation of the present conditions of world equilibrium, let us look well into each other's eyes. I perfectly understand that the satisfied nations may be in-

clined to consider such means of insuring their present
opulence and supremacy. But that is not idealism. It is the
spirit of lucre.[38]

In this, Mussolini's first official statement on
international affairs, we already have the fore-
bodings of his future policies with respect to the
League of Nations and to colonial expansion.
What he then announced as the leader of a small
group that was about to be ignominiously beaten
at the elections of November 16, 1919, he has fully
carried out as the dictator of a state militarized by
his will to a point far beyond that of pre-war Germany and Austria which he was then denouncing.
A final justification of the war in the first Fascist
program of March 23, 1919, is to be found in the
following statement:

The War . . . . has brought us negative and positive advantages. Negative in that it has prevented the Hohenzollerns, the Habsburgs and the others from establishing their
domination over the world. . . . . Positive in that none of the
victorious nations are reactionary. All nations are marching
in the direction of an ever more powerful political and economic democracy.[39]

If fascism, on the morrow of the World War, was
already or rather still warlike, it was not yet dictatorial. In a manifesto which is neither referred
to in Mussolini's *Autobiography* nor reproduced in
the official collection of his *Works and Speeches*,
but which is undeniably authentic, the leader of

[38] *Ibid.*, p. 372.   [39] *Ibid.*, p. 371.

the young Fascist group, on the eve of the elections of 1919, put forward an extraordinarily radical program.

Politically, he demanded universal suffrage irrespective of sex, proportional representation, the abolition of the Senate, and the meeting of a sovereign national assembly. This was democracy with a vengeance!

His social and fiscal demands were no less radical, since they included the immediate application of the eight-hour day, minimum wages, the representation of the workers in the technical management of industry, the administration by "proletarian organizations (on condition of technical and moral worthiness) of the public industries and services, the prompt and immediate satisfaction of the demands of the railroad workers," the lowering to fifty-five years of the age of the beneficiaries of social insurance, a "heavy extraordinary capital levy with graduated rates intended to bring about a partial expropriation of all private wealth," and the confiscation of all property belonging to religious corporations."[40]

These demands clearly show that in 1919 their author, still strongly under the influence of revolutionary syndicalism, was competing with his Socialist foes for the vote of the proletariat.

After his complete electoral defeat in 1919, the

[40] Trentin, *op. cit.*, p. 215.

war-weary Italian people having refused to elect to parliament a single member of this bellicose party, Mussolini changed both his political objectives and his electoral tactics. While never disowning his pride in the war and never ceasing to attack those responsible for the foreign policies of Italy, he began to soft-pedal on his former professions of republicanism and social extremism, declaring himself irreconcilably hostile to the Communists but enthusiastically favorable to advanced labor measures. On the major issues of internal policy, such as the maintenance of public order and financial reforms, he was very discreet. Fascism at the time was, in truth, more a movement than a party, an armed movement which spared no lives, either those of its foes or those of its members, and which no government dared openly to oppose. By insisting on will-power rather than on doctrine, on action more than on a program, Mussolini increased the number and the determination of his followers while reserving his own freedom in the choice of objectives and of allies. The following extract from an article he published in his paper on March 23, 1921, on the second anniversary of the foundation of fascism, defines—if it be a definition—his policy—if it be a policy:

Fascism is a great mobilization of material and moral forces. What does it propose? To govern the nation. We declare it without false modesty. And with what program? With a program calculated to insure the moral and material greatness of the Italian people. Let us be frank. What difference does it make if our program is not in opposition to but rather in accordance with that of the socialists in what concerns the technical administrative and political organization of our country? We call into action the moral and traditional values which socialism neglects or despises; but above all the Fascist spirit shuns everything that might constitute an arbitrary mortgage on a mysterious future. We do not believe in dogmatic programs, in rigid frames within which changing and complex reality should be contained and enslaved. We can afford the luxury of perfecting, of conciliating and of surpassing within ourselves those contradictions over which others lose their brains in petrifying themselves in monosyllabic affirmations or negations. We can afford the luxury of being at one and the same time aristocrats and democrats, conservatives and progressives, reactionaries and revolutionaries, law-abiding and law-transgressing, according to the circumstances of time, place, environment, in a word of "history," in which we are obliged to live and to act. Fascism is not a church; it is rather a base. It is not a party; it is a movement. It has no ready-made program to be carried out in the year 2000 for the simple reason that Fascism is every day building up the edifice of its will and of its passion.[41]

Thus free from any "arbitrary mortgage on a mysterious future," Mussolini joined hands with the government block and, allying himself with the Nationalists, went to the polls in May, 1921. As a result, he entered the Chamber of Deputies at the head of thirty-five Fascists who had no mind and no will but his own. Thirty-five members in a house of five hundred and thirty-five might well

[41] *Œuvres et discours*, III, 150–51.

be held to be an insignificant minority. But counting on the training of his armed bands who spread terror all over the country and on the weakness of the government, Mussolini at once addressed the legislature in the tone of a master, to the applause of his Nationalist allies. Taking his seat on the extreme right of the Assembly, he began his maiden speech on June 21, 1921, with words of deliberate and provocative boldness. He declared:

> Let me tell you at the outset that with my supreme contempt for all political labels I shall here defend doctrines of reaction. I don't know in how far my speech will be parliamentary, but I know that in substance it will be frankly anti-democratic and anti-socialist. And when I say anti-socialist, I mean also anti-Giolittian, because the exchange of amorous sentiments between Giolitti[42] and the socialist parliamentary group has never been more ardent.[43]

In this speech, which was mainly an attack on the conciliatory foreign policy of Count Sforza, Mussolini also expressed certain definite views on internal issues. He favored the clerical policy on divorce and spoke with unexpected respect of the Vatican. "I declare here," he said, "that the Latin and imperial tradition of Rome is represented today by Catholicism."[44]

While advocating advanced labor legislation, he repudiated all forms of state socialism in terms

[42] The prime minister with whose support he had been elected.

[43] *Œuvres et discours*, III, 165.

[44] *Ibid.*, p. 184.

more categorical perhaps than any that had been heard in any parliament for at least half a century. He said:

> Let the state give us a police capable of protecting honest folk against criminals. Let it give us a system of well organized justice, an army ready for all emergencies and a foreign policy adequate to our national necessities. Everything else, not excluding secondary education, should be left to individual initiative. If you wish to save the state, you must abolish the collectivist state such as it has been bequeathed to us by the War, and return to the state as advocated by the liberal school of Manchester.[45]

He concluded this extraordinary harangue by offering to disband his armed supporters if his enemies were prepared to do likewise. Whatever its sincerity, this offer was neither accepted nor made good. On the contrary, Mussolini gained ever greater control over the country by developing and leading his armed bands by whom he now came to be saluted as the Duce. It is true that the revolutionary and socialistic organizations, on the other hand, likewise continued their agitation, staging political strikes and generally paralyzing the economic life of the community. This circumstance, which is always put forward by the Fascists as the justification of their increasingly violent action and of their so-called "punitive expeditions," is generally questioned by their liberal opponents. The latter declare that the worst was

[45] *Ibid.*, p. 186.

over when on October 26, 1922, Mussolini, who, on September 20, had formally repudiated his past republicanism and proclaimed his loyalty to the House of Savoy, finally ordered his march on Rome.

Whatever degree of revolutionary violence prevailed in Italy on the eve of these events, there is no doubt that the country at large was ripe for a coup d'état. To quote but one witness, who can certainly not be accused of partiality for the Fascist view, this is how Don Sturzo describes the state of affairs prevailing in the summer of 1922:

What springs to the eye is that here was a psychological phenomenon which can only be likened to the indefinable cases of mass-suggestion, such as the unreasoning panic that sometimes seizes crowds. . . . . Italy became a prey to suggestion, to unreasoning fear and unreasoning hope—the fear of Bolshevism, when Bolshevism had been overcome two years before after the occupation of the factories; the hope that the energetic and intimidating action of the Fascist Irregulars would prove the one means of saving middle class economy and the constitutional State from the advance of Socialists and Popolari. This state of mind, excited by the general strike and by the parliamentary crisis in which industrial and agrarian capitalism had caught a glimpse of the peril of Socialist collaboration in the Government, kept the country in a state of agitation and under the incubus of inevitable coming events. The Fascisti, therefore, became in an increased degree the objects of Liberal approval and Government tolerance, while they continued the occupation of town halls and towns and onslaughts on Trade Unions and workers' co-operatives. The middle classes did not see the peril nor the illegality of the method of violence; they saw only the strengthening of their own side, which they confounded with the State. In point of fact, the State was losing authority and consistency, while the Government of the State was yielding up its powers to armed revolt. Between a Parliament that had failed to solve a Cabinet crisis and a Fascist mob that held the opposing parties at bay, the Government was for the mob.[46]

In the last critical moments of the pre-Fascist regime, the Prime Minister Facta resigned and then, faced with an armed uprising, decided on the proclamation of martial law. The king, however, refused to sign the decree and on October 28 intrusted Salandra, the head of the Nationalist party, with the task of forming a government. Mussolini, having let it be known that he would join no cabinet of which he was not to be the head, was sent for by the king, Salandra having declined his mission. On October 30 the Duce arrived in Rome just as the first columns of his Black Shirts were entering the city.

Fascism had triumphed. Mussolini had imposed his will. He was, if not yet an unconditional dictator, at any rate the complete master of the situation. He composed a ministry "of nationalist character" consisting of fourteen ministers and eighteen undersecretaries of state, all but three of whom, General Diaz, Admiral Thaon de Revel, and Professor Gentile, were members of the lower house. Of the ministers, only four, including Mussolini himself, who took with the presidency of the

46 *Op. cit.*, pp. 108-9.

[150]

Council the portfolio of the Interior and ad interim that of Foreign Affairs, were Fascists. The army and the navy were intrusted to nonpartisan military men. The other departments were distributed among the Popolari (2), the Liberals of the Right (2), the Democrats (2), the Nationalists (1), and the Social-Democrats (1). Of the undersecretaries, nine were Fascists, four Popolari, two Social-Democrats, two Nationalists, and one a Liberal of the Right.

In his *Autobiography*, Mussolini writes: "I discarded . . . . the idea of a Fascist dictatorship, because I wanted to give to the country the impression of a normal life free from the selfish exclusiveness of a party."[47] The spirit which animated this government and especially its chief is well illustrated by the speech made by Mussolini when he addressed the Chamber of Deputies for the first time as their leader, on November 16, 1922. He began by declaring:

> I could have made of this dull and gray hall a bivouac for corpses. I could have nailed up the doors of parliament and have established an exclusively Fascist government. I could have done those things, but—at least for a time—I did not do them.[48]

Having very briefly outlined his program, he concluded by declaring:

> GENTLEMEN: From further communications you will know the Fascist programme in its details. I do not want, so long

[47] P. 193.   [48] *Ibid.*, p. 197.

as I can avoid it, to rule against the Chamber; but the Chamber must feel its own position. That position opens the possibility that it may be dissolved in two days or in two years. We ask full powers because we want to assume full responsibility. Without full powers you know very well that we couldn't save one lira—I say one lira. We do not want to exclude the possibility of voluntary co-operation, for we will cordially accept it, if it comes from deputies, senators, or even from competent private citizens. Every one of us has a religious sense of our difficult task. The Country cheers us and waits. We will give it not words but facts. We formally and solemnly promise to restore the budget to health. And we will restore it. We want to make a foreign policy of peace, but at the same time one of dignity and steadiness. We will do it. We intend to give the Nation a discipline. We will give it. Let none of our enemies of yesterday, of to-day, of to-morrow cherish illusions in regard to our permanence in power. Foolish and childish illusions, like those of yesterday![49]

The full powers Mussolini asked for from the House were promptly granted and his declaration approved by three hundred and six votes against one hundred and sixteen. The Senate followed suit with a unanimous vote of confidence. Thus, called to office by the king and formally supported by a strong parliamentary majority, the Duce could in a sense look upon himself as the constitutional head of a democratic government. That he did not, however, so regard himself or at least that he did not hold his powers to be based solely on the free consent of the governed, his subsequent administration was clearly to show.

[49] *Ibid.*, p. 198.

From 1922 until the present day, every important act of the Italian government in internal affairs has tended to prepare, then to establish, and, finally, to maintain the absolute dictatorship of its head. Step by step, all non-Fascists were eliminated from the ministry, the composition of the legislature modified by laws which have tended to make of it a mere sounding board for the eloquence of its master, the king deprived of his constitutional rights, the civil service purged of all its members who refused to display subserviency to the regime, the army subordinated to his sole will, the liberty of the press first restricted and then abolished, and all other constitutional liberties of the individual ruthlessly suppressed.

The story of the gradual but rapid eclipse of liberal democracy in Italy has often been told.[50] Although its historians interpret its successive episodes very differently, some with boastful pride, some with apologetic reluctance, and some with raging indignation, all arrive substantially at the same conclusion. For the Fascists, this story is that of the glorious rise of a new empire, endowing itself and the whole world with an entirely novel and fruitful political philosophy. Their enemies, on the contrary, depict it as the resurrection of tyranny which, by depriving the Italian

[50] Cf., for instance, the various Fascist and non-Fascist writings quoted above.

people of all freedom and of all dignity and Europe of all confidence and of all security, is bound to end in disaster. On essentials, however, all are agreed. Italy is today, by the will of its Duce, a full-fledged personal dictatorship.

Already on the morrow of his advent to power, when the head of the government was still surrounded by colleagues of various parties and while he was still demanding and obtaining the support of a parliament which had been freely elected under the rule of those whom he had displaced in office, he relied on the obedience of his armed Fascists more than on his logical powers of persuasion. His conditional constitutionalism of this period is well characterized by a speech he made on March 7, 1923, when he said:

I might be asked: Why so many armed men? I declare that I wish to govern if possible with the fullest consent of the citizens. But while this consent is being achieved, nourished and strengthened, I hold at my disposal as many armed men as possible. Because it may well happen that force may help to create consent and because in any case there would be force if consent came to fail.[51]

We have seen that in the course of the last twenty years Mussolini's views, theories, and policies have undergone the most complete revolution. From extreme democracy and rabid individualism through what might be called a stage of complete political agnosticism, he has come to

[51] Trentin, *op. cit.*, p. 111.

proclaim the supreme and exclusive rights of the totalitarian state of which he is honored as the supreme and sole ruler. During the intermediary stage his agnosticism was justified by himself as realistic and wholesomely dynamic and denounced by his enemies as cynically opportunist. Today, although his critics are as bitter and his friends as enthusiastic as ever, and although there obviously can less than ever be any reconciliation between them, on one point at least all controversy has been silenced. Mussolini himself has so clearly defined himself as the enemy of all individual liberty and as the champion of the omnipotent state, that there is no room for any further polemics as to his real position. A few final quotations from his exposition of the Fascist doctrine as he penned it himself for the Italian encyclopedia will suffice to show him in his true light as the unqualified foe of all liberal democracy:

The Fascist philosophy, anti-individualistic, is for the state; it is for the individual in so far as he harmonizes himself with the state, universal conscience and will of man in his historical existence. Fascism is opposed to classical Liberalism which was born of a need for reaction against absolutism, has terminated its historical mission since the state has become the conscience and the will itself of the people. Liberalism denied the state in the interests of the individual; Fascism reaffirms the state as his true reality and if liberty shall be the attribute of the real man and not of the abstract dummy of individualistic liberty, then Fascism is for liberty. It is for the only liberty which can be a serious reality: liberty of the state and of the individual in the state. For the Fascist, everything is in the state and nothing human and spiritual can exist nor *a fortiori* have any value outside the state. In this sense Fascism is totalitarian and the Fascist state, synthesis and unity of all value, interprets, develops and dominates the whole life of the people. . . . .

The individuals . . . . are before all and above all the state. The state is neither the number nor the sum of the individuals which form the majority of the people. In this, Fascism is opposed to democracy, for whom the people is identified with the majority of the individuals and reduced to their level. Fascism is however the purest form of democracy. If the people be considered qualitatively, as they should be, and not quantitatively, it represents the most powerful because the most ethical, the most coherent and the truest idea, as the conscience and will of the small number and even of one alone as an ideal which seeks for realization in the conscience and will of all. . . . .

It is not the nation which creates the state. . . . . On the contrary, the nation is created by the state which gives the people conscious of its own moral unity a common will and consequently an effective existence. . . . .

The Fascist state . . . . is a force, but a spiritual force, a force in which all the forms of the moral and intellectual life of man are summed up. It can therefore not be limited to mere function of order and protection, as was the wish of Liberalism. . . . . It is the soul of the soul.

Fascism breaks down and rejects all democratic ideologies in their theoretical assumptions as well as in their practical applications. Fascism denies that numbers, just because they are numbers, can rule over human society; it denies that numbers, ascertained by periodical consultations, can govern; it asserts the irremediable, fruitful and beneficent inequality of men who cannot be made equal by any extrinsic and mechanical device such as universal suffrage. Democratic régimes may be defined as such in which the people are from time to time given the illusion of sovereignty, whereas real and effective sovereignty resides in other, often irresponsible and secret forces. Democracy is a kingless régime endowed with very many kings who are often more exclusive, more tyrannical and more ruinous than a sole king, even if a tyrant. . . . .

Fascism rejects in Democracy the conventional lie of political equality, the spirit of collective irresponsibility and the myth of happiness and indefinite progress. But if democracy may be otherwise understood, that is to say if democracy means the refusal to exclude the people from the state, then Fascism may be defined as "organized, centralized, authoritarian democracy."

As against Liberal doctrines, Fascism is in a state of complete opposition, in the political as well as in the economic sphere. One should not exaggerate . . . . the importance of Liberalism in the last century and make of it a religion of humanity for all present and future times, whereas it was only one of the many doctrines of that century. Liberalism enjoyed only fifteen years of favor. It was born in 1830, as a reaction against the Holy Alliance. . . . . Now Liberalism is on the point of closing the doors of its deserted temple, as the peoples feel that its agnosticism in economic matters, its indifferentism in politics and in morals would bring about, as it has already done, the certain ruin of states. That is why all the political experiments of the contemporary world are anti-Liberal and the desire to exile them from history is supremely ridiculous; as if history was a hunting preserve for Liberalism and professors, as if Liberalism was the last and incomparable word in civilization.

The fact that Fascism denies Socialism, Democracy and Liberalism should not lead one to believe that it intends to bring the world back to what it was before 1789. . . . . One never goes backwards. . . . . The Fascist idea of authority has nothing in common with the police state. A party which governs a nation in a totalitarian fashion is a fact new in history. . . . . If we assume that the nineteenth century was the century of Socialism, of Liberalism, of Democracy, it is not said that the twentieth century shall also be the century of Socialism, of Liberalism and of Democracy. Political doctrines come and go. Peoples remain. One can believe that the present century is the century of authority, a century of the "Right," a Fascist century; and if the nineteenth century was the century of the individual (Liberalism means individualism), one may think that the present century is a "collective" century and consequently the century of the state.[52]

It is not our purpose to comment at length on these quotations. Although written in the style of those philosophical professors whom Mussolini loves to deride and who might not find it all too difficult to discover and to reveal some of the hidden sources of mirth which it contains, the intentions of its author were obviously political and not philosophical. When one has denied one's own people all their rights, including that of governing themselves, one clearly owes them at least an explanation. We have read the Duce's explanation. Whatever our own views, we may readily admit with him that if his people's destiny is neither individual happiness nor indefinite progress, but statehood as he assumes, then a totalitarian state governed by a single individual, of whom he implies himself that he is the qualitatively highest incarnation of his people's virtues, may well be their salvation, their cure, or their funeral.

We doubt whether after reading the above-quoted discourse on the metaphysics of fascism any democratically or liberally inclined individual will feel that his case is lost. If anyone is refuted

[52] *Le Fascisme* (Paris, 1933), pp. 19 ff.

[158]

by the Duce's arguments, it is the Socialist Mussolini of the Avanti, the democratic Mussolini of 1919, the agnostic Mussolini of 1921, and the liberal doctrinaire of his maiden speech, who have obviously all four surrendered their past convictions into the omnipotent hands of their authoritarian successor. Moreover, it is, of course, not on its metaphysics that history will judge fascism but on its accomplishments.

On these it is as yet too early to pass final judgment. That the Italian people had already paid a high price for the internal order that has undoubtedly been improved, and for the external prestige that has been reaped on foreign battlefields is certain. Whether that price, in personal liberty and dignity, in national blood and treasure, and in international confidence be deemed negligible or excessive, will depend not only on one's estimate of the avoided dangers of revolution, of the advantages of intensified national energy, and on one's forecast as to future evolution, but also on one's sense of values.

Mussolini—it is the point on which his words and acts show the greatest consistency in the course of the last twenty years—is temperamentally fond of force, of violence, of danger, and of war. That those whose conception of civilization is at the very opposite pole from his, whose ideals are on the contrary freedom, justice, security, and peace,

should disagree with him even if—or, rather, especially if—he should be successful in attaining
his aims, is obvious. Our purpose, however, is not
to assess values but to explain happenings. Whatever we may think of Mussolini's dictatorship, its
establishment and maintenance for the duration
of already nearly half a generation is a historical
fact of the first importance and one which could
not be understood except as a product of the World
War.

Benito Mussolini had been in power for over ten
years when he was joined in the Pantheon of
contemporary dictators by one who was to become
even more powerful—Adolf Hitler.

We have seen in our last chapter how under the
pressure of military reverses and as the direct result of the diplomacy of President Wilson Germany
became a republic in 1918, and how of her own free
will she adopted a democratic constitution in July,
1919. One will never know whether this liberal
constitution could have brought Germany stability and political contentment had the external
and internal circumstances been more favorable.
What we do know, however, is that these circumstances could hardly have been less so. And what
we know also is that, having experienced three
presidential elections and over twenty ministerial
changes in the course of fourteen years, the German

people in 1933 gave themselves over to a complete dictatorship without much resistance and with no violent reactions.[53]

The unfavorable external circumstances were the immediate and inevitable consequences of the Treaty of Versailles. That unfortunate agreement, if it may be so called, was not unusually severe in its territorial clauses if we compare it either with past treaties of peace imposed on a defeated invader who had waged almost the whole war on the territory of his victorious victims, or with the other treaties of 1919 which dismembered Austria-Hungary or, especially, with the Treaty of Brest-Litovsk imposed on Russia by Germany in 1917 and which foreshadowed that which she doubtless would have imposed on the Allies had they been defeated. We have it on the unimpeachable authority of Herr Hitler himself that this was the general feeling in Germany in the years immediately following the conclusion of the Treaty of Versailles. In recalling his first efforts at arousing the indignation of his fellow-countrymen against their victors, he wrote:

At that time (1920) a public mass meeting . . . . summoned for the discussion of the Treaty of Versailles was taken as an attack on the Republic and as the expression of reactionary,

[53] Cf. Friedrich Stampfer, *Die vierzehn Jahre der ersten Deutschen Republik* (Karlsbad, 1936); Arthur Rosenberg, *A History of the German Republic*, trans. from the German (London, 1936); and Frederick L. Schuman, *Hitler and the Nazi Dictatorship* (London, 1936).

if not of monarchical views. The very first sentence contain-
ing a criticism of Versailles was sure to call forth from the
audience the stereotyped cry of "What about Brest-Litovsk?
Brest-Litovsk!" This the crowd yelled again and again until
they gradually became hoarse or until the orator finally gave
up the attempt at convincing them.[54]

But if the territorial terms of the treaty were
not, and were not even in Germany at first held
to be, unduly harsh, its financial and military provisions no less than the mode of its negotiation
were undoubtedly such as to discredit and to
weaken the German government which had been
obliged to accept them and which for an indefinite period was to act as the executor of a hostile foreign will. How much wiser it would have
been to welcome the representatives of a contrite
republican Germany to Paris as had been welcomed
to Vienna a century before the representatives of
a contrite monarchical France! And how much
wiser, both more generous and more profitable, it
would have been to come to terms with them as
with the victims of a common aggressive autocratic and militaristic enemy who had been defeated by the victors and repudiated by a mis-
guided and repentant people! Instead, the statesmanship which prevailed at Versailles, under the
implacable leadership of Clemenceau, tended permanently to humiliate, to ruin, and to disarm an
already prostrate nation and thereby to render

[54] Hitler, *Mein Kampf* (42d ed.; Munich, 1933), p. 519.

well-nigh impossible the task of its new and in-
experienced government.

What Clemenceau had begun in 1919 with the
partly active and partly reluctant connivance of
Lloyd George and in the face of the intermittent
but unsuccessful opposition of Wilson, Poincaré
pursued alone in 1923. By ordering his army to
invade the Ruhr district with the intention of
obliging the German government more faithfully
to fulfil its obligations on a reparation's debt on
the total of which the disunited Allies had not
yet been able to agree, this sincere republican-
democrat of France became the most effective
promoter of the cause of dictatorship beyond the
Rhine. As Hitler wrote shortly afterward:

> The French invasion of the Ruhr opened up the greatest
> possibilities for the future of Germany both in the field of
> foreign politics and internally. An important part of our
> people, who, under the continuous influence of a mendacious
> press, persisted in seeing in France the champion of progress
> and liberty, were brutally cured of their illusion. As the
> year 1914 had dispelled the dream of international solidarity
> in the heads of our German workers and had suddenly
> brought them back into the real world of eternal struggle, in
> which everywhere one being feeds on another and the life of
> the stronger is insured by the death of the weaker, so also the
> Spring of 1923. When France finally carried out her threats
> and began at first very cautiously and hesitatingly to occupy
> the German coal fields, a great, a decisive hour of destiny
> had come for Germany.[55]

[55] *Ibid.*, p. 769.

Not only had Poincaré convinced the disarmed German people that no international guaranties but only a national army could protect the integrity of their soil, but he had unwittingly, by opening the locks of monetary inflation in Germany, initiated the great social revolution which was to ruin the middle classes and to throw them into the arms of Hitler.

These middle classes, with the support of the mass of the workers enrolled in the ranks of the very moderate Social Democratic party, were seeking to govern republican Germany against the communistic revolutionaries of the left and the monarchical reactionaries of the right. As long as they were tolerably prosperous and as long as their labor allies were tolerably secure in their employment, the liberal republic was safe. But when the whole social structure which had hardly begun to recover from the shocks of the war was again dislocated by inflation and economic disaster, the political life of the country became more and more feverish and the authority of the government more and more uncertain.

The retreat of the French troops in the autumn of 1923, and the more conciliatory policies of the Briand-Stresemann era, aided by the vast influx of foreign capital, once more restored a measure of order and of relative contentment. But the order and the contentment proved precarious and dependent upon the course of economic events. With the outbreak of the world-crisis which followed upon the panic in Wall Street of October, 1929, the fate of liberal German democracy was doomed.

Its final downfall in 1923 had been predicted and prepared for ever since the end of the war, by a man whose name we have already had occasion to mention, but whose history, character, and program we must now consider with some care. When compared with his Italian fellow-dictator, who has achieved a similar position of unquestioned authority and who bases it on a comparable, if not identical, social philosophy, Adolf Hitler's chief distinguishing feature is intellectual consistency. Whereas Mussolini, as we have seen, repeatedly and radically modified his political views to adapt them to the changing exigencies of his career, Hitler was already a ruthless rational critic of democracy and a thoroughgoing apostle of nationalistic dictatorship when he was still very far removed from the seat of supreme power.

We know it mainly thanks to the circumstance—exceptionally fortunate for the historian—that on April 1, 1924, more than ten years before becoming his country's leader-chancellor, Hitler spent nine months in a Bavarian prison to which he had been sentenced for five years as guilty of an armed nationalistic uprising against the state. During his detention, which was to be both shortened and alleviated by the leniency with which his patriotic crime was regarded by the authorities, he began at the age of thirty-five drafting his autobiography which was to be published in two volumes under the title of *Mein Kampf*.[56] The first volume, dealing with the author's experiences before, during, and after the World War until the beginning of 1920, appeared in 1925. In the second, which was to be published two years later, it told the story and expounded the program of the National-Socialist movement from 1920 until 1926.

It is quite obvious that this extraordinary work, which is rightly regarded as the gospel of the Nazi religion, was written with a political much more than with a historical intention. Its author, even when recalling and commenting on his past, is not looking backward so much as forward to his future, which was already inseparably bound up, in his own mind, with that of his party and of his country. Although it should, therefore, not be read as a scientific monograph, it is an essentially valuable source of information for the true understanding of the advent of dictatorship in Germany. Here was a political agitator not yet regarded as the sole leader of an as yet small revolutionary party, who in all intellectual independence explains how and why he came to espouse the cause and to formulate

[56] Stampfer, *op. cit.*, pp. 342 ff.; Rosenberg, *op. cit.*, pp. 213 ff.; Schuman, *op. cit.*, pp. 39 ff.

the policies which he some years later imposed on his country as its unquestioned master.

As we are not here interested in the tactics nor even in the strategy of public agitation, subversive plotting, political alliances, and electoral combinations by which Hitler succeeded in his endeavors, but only in his general program of action, nothing could be more enlightening than the study of *Mein Kampf*. Whatever we may think of its author's sincerity and frankness, the circumstances and the very date of its first publication insure its value for our purposes. Thus, even if we should not be convinced that Hitler was converted to his ideals of dictatorship in Vienna prior to the World War, as he would lead us to believe in one of his first chapters, there is no doubt that, writing in defense of those ideals in 1924, he wished them to be known as his, long before he could reasonably expect them to be realized in his own person. Let us therefore carefully consider the message contained in *Mein Kampf*—in our opinion by far the most important book that has appeared in any country since the war. We must of course consult the unabridged German edition, since our quest is for the essence of Hitler's philosophy as revealed to his own people, and not only for those elements of it which he deemed it opportune to present to the French and English reading public.

Born in 1889 as the son of a minor Austrian customhouse official on the Austro-German frontier, Adolf Hitler declared that he emerged from his earliest primary-school days as a predestined orator, as an intelligent student of history, and above all as an ardent nationalist.[57] The object of his patriotism was, however, not Austria-Hungary, its land, its people, its institutions, or its dynasty, but the German-speaking community, the *deutsches Volkstum*. Thus, what he calls his nationalism inspired in him not the ambition to enter the Austrian government service in accordance with his father's wishes, but, on the contrary, the revolutionary desire to see the dissolution of the Habsburg Empire and the emancipation of its German subjects. He writes:

> Who could study . . . . German history without becoming an enemy of the state whose traditional rulers so fatally influenced the destiny of the nation? Who could feel any loyalty to a dynasty which, in the past as in the present, had always betrayed and was constantly betraying the interests of the German people for its own pitiful advantages. Hadn't we children already learnt that this Austrian state had no love for us Germans and could have none.[58]

Whereas Hitler thus assures us that his national views date from his earliest childhood on the Austro-German border, his opinions on social and economic problems were first shaped by his adolescent experiences in Vienna. Having lost his father and his mother and being obliged to shift for him-

[57] Hitler, *op. cit.*, pp. 3, 8 ff. [58] *Ibid.*, p. 13.

self from the age of sixteen, he repaired to the
Austrian capital in the hope of being admitted to
an art school. Disappointed in this, he was obliged to earn his meager living as a painter in the
building trade. Here he came into contact with the
human misery of an urban proletariat, with trade-
unionism, with socialistic agitation and tyranny,
and with bourgeois indifference.

What shocked him most in the lot of the working
classes of Vienna was the fact that the economic
and social conditions under which they were compelled to live deprived them not only of all security, but especially also of all pride of race and
of all respect for authority. Thus he writes:

> The problem of the "nationalization" of a people is first
> of all the problem of the creation of wholesome social sur-
> roundings as the basis for the education of the individual. He
> alone who, through education and schooling, has learnt to
> know the cultural, the economic and above all the political
> greatness of his own fatherland may and also will gain that
> inner pride which springs from the consciousness of being
> privileged to belong to such a people. And I can fight only
> for what I love, love only what I respect and respect only what
> I at least know.[59]

Trade-unions he was led by his personal experiences both to appreciate as necessities in the face
of the blind selfishness of the bourgeois-entre-
preneur class and to loathe as the instruments
of political tyranny. The bourgeoisie is made re-

[59] *Ibid.*, p. 34.

sponsible not only for their existence but also for
their unfortunate subordination to the Socialist
party, which came to exploit them for its political
purposes.[60]

For the Socialist party itself Hitler professes
the most violent horror, as for the incarnation of
all evil. Through its mendacious and terrorist
methods it deceives and crushes the individual.
Through the international doctrine of the class
struggle it threatens all national units. Through its
constant appeal to selfishness and hatred it tends
to the very destruction of all human society. As
he became familiar with the authors of its doctrines, with the inspirers of its press, and with its
political leaders, it gradually dawned upon him, he
declares, that they were almost all Jews. He
writes: "In the study of Jewry alone is to be found
the key to the understanding of the inner and true
intentions of socialism."[61]

Little by little he came to see in Austrian Jewry
the pernicious influence responsible not only for
the rise of socialism but also for the constant struggle against the policies of the German Reich. Thus
anti-Semitism and pan-Germanism, each inspiring
and exciting the other, became his dominant creed.

In the course of his stay in Vienna his growing
interest in politics led him to pay an occasional
visit to the Austrian parliament. Although he had

[60] *Ibid.*, p. 51.   [61] *Ibid.*, p. 54.

at first rather welcomed the struggle of the Social
ists for the introduction of universal suffrage as a
menace to the hated Habsburg regime,[62] he later
came to see that its parliamentary results would
be fatal for the supremacy of Germanism in Austria.[63] Furthermore, he perceived in "Western democracy the precursor of Marxism which could
flourish only on a democratic basis."

He therefore came to add democracy and parliamentarism to the Habsburg dynasty, to socialism,
and to Jewry in the growing list of his hatreds.
Hitler's critique of democracy as elaborated in the
first volume of *Mein Kampf* well deserves our attention here. Even if it should not have been suggested to him solely by his study of Austrian parliamentarism, as he intimates, it shows that, in
1924 in any case, that is long before he became
Germany's Führer, he had already adopted and
proclaimed the virtues of the Führer principle. In
discussing the working of democratic politics, as
he had occasion to observe them in Vienna, he
writes:

The earliest and most substantial fruit for reflection was
the obvious absence of all responsibility of any individual
person.

Parliament takes any kind of a decision however devastating its consequences—nobody is responsible therefor, nobody
can be held to account for it. For can one claim that it is assumption of responsibility if after a catastrophe the guilty

[62] *Ibid.*, p. 39.   [63] *Ibid.*, p. 82.

government hands in its resignation? Or if the coalition is broken up or even if parliament is dissolved?

Can a fluctuating majority of men ever be made responsible for anything?

Is not the very concept of responsibility bound up with the individual person?

In practice, can the leading members of a government ever be called to account for policies shaped and carried out solely according to the will and preference of a multitude of men?

Or does the task of the leading statesman consist not in the formulation of creative ideas and plans, but rather in the art of convincing a herd of idiots of the excellence of his projects, in order to gain their consent thereto by beggary?

Is a statesman to be judged just as much by his ability to convince as by the statesmanlike vision displayed in the conception and in the execution of great plans?

Is a leader to be held a failure just because he does not succeed in winning over to a given idea the majority of a gang brought together by more or less reprehensible devices?

Has such a gang ever understood an idea before its greatness was revealed by its success?

Is not every act of genius in this world the living protest of genius against the dull indolence of the mass?

But what is the statesman to do if he does not succeed in gaining the favor of this gang for his measures by flattery? Shall he buy their favor?

Or shall he, in the face of the stupidity of his fellow-citizens, refrain from carrying out the measures recognized as vitally necessary? Shall he withdraw or shall he remain in power?

Is it not inevitable in such a case that a man of real character will become engaged in an insoluble conflict between intelligence and decency or rather simple honesty?

Who is to trace the frontier between one's duty to the community and the obligations of personal honor?

Must not every true leader revolt against such a degradation to the level of the political profiteer and conversely

must not every profiteer feel called upon to become a politician, since the final responsibility never rests with him but
with some kind of an unseizable band?

Does not the majority principle in our parliaments necessarily result in the destruction of the idea of true leadership?

Can one believe that progressive ideas in this world can
spring from the brain of majorities and not originate in the
heads of individuals?[64]

It would be possible, but hardly necessary, to
prolong this quotation. It suffices to show the impatience of a born leader with the necessary compromises and concessions inherent in all democratic governments of the parliamentary type.
Summing up his views on democracy in general,
he writes:

It is by reason of its very character that this kind of democracy has become the instrument of the race whose hidden
motives make of it the foe of daylight at present and for all
times. The Jew alone can extoll an institution which is as
unclean and as untrue as he is himself.

As opposed to this institution, there stands the true Ger-
manic democracy, with its free choice of a leader and with
the latter's duty to assume full responsibility for its deeds
and omissions. This democracy knows no majority votes on
special questions but only the selection of an individual ac-
countable for his actions with his whole fortune and with his
very life.[65]

Thus, according to his own confessions published
in 1924, Adolf Hitler had already before the outbreak of the World War elaborated in all its essential features the social philosophy of which he is

[64] *Ibid.*, pp. 85 ff.   [65] *Ibid.*, p. 99.

today the chief exponent in the field of practical politics.

If we are to believe *Mein Kampf*, the war brought the Führer two further revelations, of unequal importance, but both significant when considered from the point of view of his future policies.

The first of these revelations relates to war itself. That even prior to 1914 internationalism and pacifism should have had no attractions for Hitler was at least probable in view of his pan-German ambitions, of his pride of race, of his cult of the state, of his belief in personal authority, and of his indifference to individual liberty. But that he should rejoice in war, as in the necessary and beneficent means of insuring the triumph of his own people, seems to have been the result of his personal war and post-war experiences. It is worth noting that on no other subject are his opinions less rational and as self-contradictory as on that of war and peace.

On the one hand, he of course indignantly repudiates both for the German government and for the German people the responsibility for the war of 1914. But, on the other, he blames the German government chiefly for not having chosen a more opportune moment for striking the first blow.[66] As for the German people and as for himself, he writes:

[66] *Ibid.*, p. 176.

If the Austrian government had formulated the ultimatum [addressed to Serbia] in other, milder terms, it would not have modified the position in the least, except possibly that the government would have been swept away by a wave of popular indignation. In the eyes of the masses, the tone of the ultimatum was far too considerate and not in any way too exacting or too brutal. He who denies that today is either a forgetful idiot or a deliberate liar.

Heaven knows the War of 1914 was not imposed on the masses but on the contrary demanded by the whole people. One wished to bring the general uncertainty to an end. It is only thus that one can understand that more than 2 million German men and boys volunteered to take part in the struggle. . . . .

As for myself, those hours were as an emancipation from the most irritating impressions of my youth. Even today I am not ashamed to confess that, overcome by a storm of enthusiasm, I fell on my knees and thanked heaven out of an overflowing heart that I had been granted the joy of living at this time.[67]

The man who, ten years after the World War, having himself spent four years in the trenches and witnessed the infinite horror thereof, could speak in such terms of the outbreak of the major catastrophe in the history of mankind, can obviously not be called a pacifist. When he comes to discuss pacifism itself, he does so with more apprehensive and bitter hostility even than skepticism. He writes:

If anyone really wished for the triumph of the pacifist idea in the world, he should be obliged by all means to advocate its conquest by Germany. He should have to do so because if the contrary was to happen, the last pacifist might

[67] *Ibid.*, pp. 176 ff.

well die with the last German, it being unfortunately unlikely that the rest of mankind would succumb to this unnatural and irrational folly as readily as our own people. Willy-nilly one would therefore have to go to war in order to realize the idea of peace. It was this and nothing else that the American world savior Wilson had planned. Such at least was the belief of our German dreamers and thus the trick succeeded.[68]

It would be difficult in less words to express more repugnance for the ideal of a peacefully organized universe. Like socialism, democracy, and parliamentarism, so peace is for Hitler nothing but an invention of Jewry for the corruption and deceit of the sounder and stronger races. Of these races, the German has the biological right not only to include in its own national frontiers all its German-speaking neighbors, but further to secure by conquest, if need be, the necessary territory and natural resources in colonies and elsewhere to allow for its normal expansion.

The other lesson which the World War taught Hitler was that of the importance of mass propaganda. Were it not for the role which this propaganda was to play in his scheme of government, it would not be worth while to mention it here. But given his belief in dictatorial leadership and his contempt for public opinion, propaganda, truthful or mendacious, but always ruthless, was, in his view, as it has become under his rule, more than a mere instrument of government, a fundamental institu-

[68] *Ibid.*, p. 315.

tion calculated to allow one supreme will to dominate a misled but consenting nation.

The political philosophy expounded in *Mein Kampf* is in all its essential features that which is being applied in Germany today. The aggressive German nationalism and the passionate and unspeakably cruel anti-Semitism which Hitler had inherited from his early Vienna days were sentiments and policies very similar to those expressed and advocated by his two Austrian models, Freiherr von Schönerer and the burgomaster Lueger.[69] The anticapitalistic, antisocialistic, antiparliamentary, and antidemocratic tendencies also seem to have sprung from Austrian sources, as they had obviously been shared, although in varying degrees of intensity, by many German and Austrian predecessors. The idea of a personal dictatorship, on the other hand, seems to have been both more recent and more original with Hitler. It was doubtless born of a reaction against irresponsible parliamentarism and possibly also of military discipline experienced during the war, of a sort of kingless monarchism, and of the recent example of Mussolini of whom he wrote in the second volume of *Mein Kampf:* "I confess it frankly, I conceived the deepest admiration for the great man to the South of the Alps whose ardent love of his people

---

[69] *Ibid.*, pp. 107 ff; Theodor Heuss, *Hitlers Weg* (Berlin, 1932), p. 25.

refused to allow him to compromise with the internal foes of Italy but led him to seek their destruction by all means and methods."[70]

As for Hitler's hatred of pacifism and belief in the inevitability and excellence of war, they were clearly the children of his war experiences which led him to count on force alone for the promotion of his national aims.

It would take far more time and space than we have at our disposal to recall the story of Hitler's almost miraculous advent to power, from his liberation from the birthplace of *Mein Kampf* in December, 1924, to his accession to the chancellorship in Berlin in January, 1933.[71] It is the story of an uncannily effective public orator, of an astonishingly clever organizer, and of an exceptionally successful political leader, who, in less than ten years, completely conquered the soul, or at any rate, mastered the will, of the German people.

In the course of his popular campaigning he was entirely unhampered by any censorship or by any of the other restrictions on the freedom of the press, of speech, and of assembly, which he promptly imposed upon his enemies once he came into power.

[70] P. 774.

[71] The story has often been told. Cf. especially the above-quoted works by Stampfer, Rosenberg, and Schuman. See also Konrad Heiden, *Hitler, a Biography* (London, 1936), perhaps the most discriminating of the many Hitler biographies which have been published in the course of the last few years.

But while thus making full use of the liberal institutions he was bent on overthrowing, and while engaging in the parliamentary tactics which he had so severely condemned, he never lost sight of nor wavered from his ultimate aim. And that aim, which he has today achieved, is precisely that which he publicly announced in *Mein Kampf*.

When on August 17, 1934, Hitler, speaking in Hamburg, announced the reasons which had compelled him at once to assume the powers vested in President von Hindenburg until his death, he declared:

> Even my most vicious maligners will admit I never wavered or faltered in this fifteen-year fight. Whether at liberty or in jail, I stuck to my colours, which today are the flag of the Reich. Nor can they prove that I committed or omitted a single political act for reason of personal gain, and they must finally admit that this battle has not been without success; out of a movement of humble origin there has emerged a victorious revolution, one that has brought the German people a new and better standing, both at home and abroad.
>
> I gladly assume responsibility for such mistakes as may be charged to me. They fall within the scope of human frailty. But I have never committed a deed or an act which I was convinced would not redound to the benefit of the German people. Ever since I first stood in the thick of this political battle, I have been actuated by only one motive—so help me God—only one thought: Germany![72]

Even the most passionate critics of the German leader-chancellor and even the most unjustly

[72] Schuman, *op. cit.*, p. 466.

treated of his countless innocent victims will not find much to quarrel with in this dramatic statement. His aims may seem as contemptible as his methods are avowedly ruthless and inhuman, but one can hardly accuse him either of personal self-seeking or of any lack of fidelity to the cause which ever since 1924 he publicly announced as being his.

That triumphant national-socialism is a product of the World War no less than Italian fascism and Russian bolshevism is too obvious to need reassertion. Without the events of 1914–18, Hitler would doubtless still be an obscure and discontented subject of the Habsburgs, and the German people would certainly still be the loyal subjects of the Hohenzollerns. Without them democracy would not have been proclaimed and therefore could not have been challenged and overthrown in either Berlin, Vienna, or Moscow. The same could be said of all the other states which adopted liberal constitutions after the war and which have repudiated them since in favor of some more or less disguised form of dictatorship.

Should we then dismiss both the temporary and premature advent of democracy and its prompt collapse in countries manifestly ill prepared for it, as a mere passing phase? Should we dismiss the whole so-called crisis of democracy as an accident of history, which history, if allowed to run its

normal course, will not fail to overcome? Even
our brief analysis of the rise of the three great
European dictatorships were to suggest such a detached optimistic view of our subject, we could not
fail to be diverted therefrom by considering the
evolution of democracy in those European countries which, having adopted liberal institutions
earlier and under less normal conditions, are still
clinging to them today.

CHAPTER V

THE EVOLUTION OF DEMOCRACY IN THE SURVIVING DEMOCRACIES

If the crisis of democracy in the contemporary world was perceived only in the rise of post-war dictatorships, we should have heard much less about it. When discussing the latter, the friends of democracy would seek for their books and articles some such titles as "Guides into Darkness," "Reactionary Tyrants," "Benighted Peoples," or "The Price of Democracy." And the admirers of autocracy would speak, not of the crisis of democracy, but of its final downfall as that of an obsolete regime.

Democracy, like every other form of government, is in a sense a means to an end. Its most enthusiastic friends extol it as the best means for the attainment of the highest of ends. For them, there can obviously be no question of a crisis of democracy. Its most radical critics, on the other hand, reject it root and branch because they both repudiate its ideals and despise its processes. When they succeed in overthrowing a democratic government or in seriously impeding its operation, they may well provoke a crisis of democracy, but they would hardly describe it as such. The overthrow of democracy or its difficulties are experienced and described as crises primarily by those who profess the same ideals as its founders, but who are led to question or to denounce its processes as unsatisfactory means for the attainment of ends held to be excellent in themselves.

That is the position in many if not in all contemporary democracies. As a matter of fact, the countless publications on democracy and its crisis which have appeared in the course of the last twenty years are for the greater part the works of British, American, and French authors who have been attracted to the subject not by their hatred of democracy but rather by their misgivings and solicitous apprehensions about its future.

In order fully to appreciate this important fact, let us consider the titles of some of the works on democracy which have appeared since the war.

In 1918: Joseph-Barthélemy, *Le Problème de la compétence dans la démocratie* (Paris).

In 1919: F. A. Cleveland, *Democracy in Reconstruction* (Boston); A. T. Hadley, *The Moral Basis of Democracy* (New Haven); W. E. Weyl, *The New Democracy* (New York); H. J. Mackinder, *Democratic Ideals and Reality* (London).

In 1920: R. Roberts, *The Unfinished Program of Democracy* (New York).

In 1921: A. T. Hadley, *The Relations between Freedom and Responsibility in the Evolution of Democratic Government* (New Haven); G. H. Chardon, *L'Organisation d'une démocratie* (Paris).

In 1922: Shailer Mathews, *The Validity of American*

THE CRISIS OF DEMOCRACY

Ideals (Cincinnati); J. Massabuau, *L'Etat contre la nation* (Paris).

In 1925: M. J. Bonn, *The Crisis of European Democracy* (New Haven; German trans., Munich); G. N. Serventi, *Ascesa della democrazia europea e prime reazioni storiche* (Rome).

In 1926: R. Hubert, *Le Principe d'autorité dans l'organisation démocratique* (Paris).

In 1928: C. Guy-Grand, *L'Avenir de la démocratie* (Paris); C. M. P. Maurras, *Les Princes des nuées* (Paris); F. A. W. Gisborne, *Democracy on Trial* (London).

In 1929: Irving Babbitt, *Democracy and Leadership* (Boston); Charles Benoist, *Les Maladies de la démocratie* (Paris); C. Delisle Burns, *Democracy, Its Defects and Advantages* (London); P. Flottes, *La Démocratie entre deux abîmes* (Paris); H. Bourgin, *Quand tout le monde est roi, la crise de la démocratie* (Paris); H. Letterlé, *Fascisme, communisme ou démocratie* (Paris); A. Zimmern, *The Prospects of Democracy* (London).

In 1930: P. Archambault, *Réalisme démocratique* (Paris); G. Deherme, *L'immense question de l'ordre* (Paris); M. Leinert, *Volksstaat oder Diktatur?* (Gotha); M. A. Pink, *A Realist Looks at Democracy* (London); Silvio Trentin, *Antidémocratie* (Paris).

In 1931: Lord Eustace Percy, *Democracy on Trial* (London).

In 1932: E. Gascoin, *Réforme de l'Etat* (Paris); H. Kraus, *The Crisis of German Democracy* (Princeton); H. G. Wells, *After Democracy* (London).

In 1933: Harold J. Laski, *Democracy in Crisis* (London); G. Leibholz, *Die Auflösung der liberalen Demokratie* (Munich); American Academy of Political and Social Science, *The Crisis of Democracy* (ed. C. N. Callender, Philadelphia).

In 1934: H. N. Brailsford, *Property or Peace* (London); J. A. Hobson, *Democracy and a Changing Civilization* (London); H. C. Hoover, *The Challenge to Liberty* (New York); W. Newbold, *Democracy, Debts and Disarmament* (London).

In 1935: Joseph-Barthélemy, *Valeur de la liberté et adaptation de la République* (Paris); American Academy of Political and Social Science, *Socialism, Fascism and Democracy* (ed. E. M. Patterson, Philadelphia); J. A. R. Marriott, *Dictatorship and Democracy* (Oxford).

In 1936: C. Sutton, *Farewell to Rousseau: A Critique of Liberal Democracy* (London); S. de Madariaga, *Anarchie ou hiérarchie, la crise de la démocratie* (Paris); O. Bauer, *Zwischen zwei Weltkriegen? Die Krise der Weltwirtschaft, der Demokratie und des Sozialismus* (Bratislava).

In 1937: Hamilton Fish Armstrong, *We or They—Two Worlds in Conflict* (New York); A. Amrein, *Volk ohne Führung* (Zurich); L. R. Franck, *Démocraties en crise* (Paris).

In 1938: E. Giraud, *La Crise de la démocratie et le renforcement du pouvoir exécutif* (Paris).

This long but far from exhaustive list of titles suffices to show that all is not well with contemporary democracy, even in the eyes of some of its staunchest supporters.[1] They may have remained faithful to its ideals, they may have forfeited none of their fervor for liberty and equality and lost none of their faith in the superiority of government by the consent of the governed. But they are anxious, uneasy, worried. They ask themselves: Is democracy, which was born in a simpler age and in smaller surroundings, adapted and adaptable to the exigencies of an industrial civilization with all its complex problems, its teeming cities, and its mighty world-states? Can it obtain of the many that they submit peacefully to the rule of the few?

[1] For a longer but still, of course, not exhaustive list of books on problems of contemporary government see the bibliography on p. 274.

Can it obtain of the masses that they select the ablest to govern them and of the ablest that they consent to serve the masses in the interest, not of the privileged few, but of the whole community? Can democracy maintain public order without resorting to violence? Can it afford to all the necessary minimum of social security without suppressing the necessary minimum of individual liberty? Can it administer the state financially so as to make both ends meet? Can it even in times of emergency so limit public expenditure as to avoid crushing its taxpayers, ruining its borrowers, and inflating its currency? Can it cope in the diplomatic and in the military field with foreign powers, even if they be dictatorially organized?

Such are the main questions which constitute if not the indictment of, at least the challenge to, democracy in the post-war world.

To study the rise of dictators is to tell of events, of happenings, often dramatic. To study the crisis of democracy in the surviving democracies, on the other hand, is to discuss this indictment or this challenge, that is, to describe a state of mind and to analyze existing uneasiness and discontent.

This existing feeling of uneasiness and discontent with the actual working of democracy may be perceived in all the surviving democracies, but it varies appreciably both in extent and in intensity from one country to another.

EVOLUTION OF DEMOCRACY

It seems most general and most acute in France, where we shall therefore consider it first. Taking account only incidentally of the strictures of the Royalists and Nationalists of the extreme right and of the Communists of the extreme left, we shall in the main confine our analysis to the views of some of those authors who in the course of the last twenty years have expressed dissatisfaction with the operation of the present republican democratic regime while remaining steadfastly faithful to the fundamental principles of 1789 as summarized by the revolutionary slogan of "liberty, equality, fraternity." These authors undoubtedly represent the vast majority of the French people, who are as passionately fond of liberty and as radically hostile to all hereditary distinctions as they are averse to any form of political absolutism, be it of the legitimist, Bonapartist, or modern Fascist type.

In seeking first to assess the extent and the intensity of popular dissatisfaction with the working of democracy in France and then to analyze its causes, we are confronted with two major difficulties. How can we form an accurate judgment of that dissatisfaction? If we were to rely only on what falls from the lips of Frenchmen of all classes or on what one may read in the press, in the periodical literature, and in the mass of recent books published on the subject, it would be difficult to understand how and why the Third Republic had survived the onslaught of the devastating criticism to which it has been subjected ever since its birth. The average Frenchman of today, when compared to almost any of his foreign contemporaries, is both exceptionally articulate and exceptionally interested in politics. And yet it is extremely rare, either in the course of casual conversation or in the course of careful reading, to come into contact with any French mind which shows any fervent admiration or even much apologetic leniency for the government of France. Two years ago, after the general elections which brought into power the present majority of the *Front populaire*, a wave of enthusiasm seemed to sweep over the country, extending even to its political institutions. But it was as short-lived as it was obviously ill founded, and today the bitterness is commensurate with the disappointed illusions. To the minority of those whose past attitude allows them to say "I told you so, what could you expect?" has today to be added the majority of those who are deprived both of that excuse and of that consolation.

The only method of extracting a word of appreciation in favor of French political institutions from the average Frenchman is to speak with praise or even without unqualified horror of the contemporary dictatorships. Then he is likely to revolt and to reply with Professor Joseph-Barthélemy:

EVOLUTION OF DEMOCRACY

I am the first to declare . . . . that French parliamentarism is far removed from perfection. But if my loyalty tends to fade away when I consider these institutions in themselves, it is immediately strengthened again when I compare them with certain others. I do not speak of regimes founded on the continuous use of methods of violence: by definition they can be but transitory. If I turn to one side, the French Chamber strikes me as superior to the Soviet; if I turn to another, I am bound to repeat after Cavour that the Chamber is preferable to any antichamber.[2]

In view of the almost universal criticism which is poured on French democracy even by the great majority of French democrats, it is well to remember that politics, much like physical health, is a topic of conversation primarily for those who have some complaint. When a man is politically content, as when he is physically well, he is likely to show more interest in almost any other subject than government or medicine. This does not imply that the average Frenchman is satisfied with the working of his democratic institutions, but it does justify us in admitting that he is less universally and less violently dissatisfied than those who make speeches and write articles and books on the crisis of democracy.

Our second difficulty relates to the immediate causes of this discontent. Why is the average Frenchman discontented with his government? What are the charges which he brings against it?

[2] Joseph-Barthélemy, *op. cit.*, 1931, p. 136.

We shall consider first the direct indictment of its failings and then seek to probe into the underlying causes. But in what order shall we present the French indictment of French democracy, since there is hardly an aspect of political life and hardly a branch of political activity which is not being challenged in France today? Without attaching undue significance to this order, let us consider the indictment in that of the relative importance of the functions of government

The most elementary duty of all governments is doubtless the establishment and maintenance of public order. Now, although life, if not all personal property, is tolerably secure in France today, the government, especially since the advent of the *Front populaire*, is very generally indicted for its inability or for its reluctance to maintain order. In 1931, M. Barthélemy was rash enough to write the following words: "I do not wish in passing to criticize the Fascist régime of M. Mussolini. I only note that Italy has fallen into an abyss of anarchy which is and which will remain foreign to France; we have not yet seen communist workmen occupying factories as if they were their masters."[3]

What was true in 1931 is unfortunately no longer true today. Although no signs of disorder are apparent to the foreigner traveling in France, there is no doubt that recent governments have failed

[3] *Op. cit.*, p. 236.

to protect the community against the aggressive action of revolutionary trade movements. This criticism, which is, of course, far more frequently voiced by the conservative press than by that which supports the *Front populaire,* may be heard more and more generally in France today.

The administration of justice is also coming to be more and more attacked by students of French political affairs. They often insist on the dangers to which the independence of the courts is exposed by reason of the insufficiency of the salaries of the judges and of the undue influence exercised by the government and through it by the legislature on their promotion. Thus M. Gascoin writes:

Even assuming the majority of our judges to be disinterested enough to forego the satisfaction of their most legitimate ambitions, the highest judicial positions, those in which the final decisions are reached by the normal process of appeal and annulment, are all the more generally entrusted to those who have succeeded in ingratiating themselves with the legislature of which the government is but a screen and which here also is the sole arbiter of the much coveted promotions.[4]

As for the question of national security, all French authors profess complete confidence in the valor and in the technical ability of the army and navy. But all admit also that it would be irrelevant to draw any conclusions therefrom in favor of

[4] E. Gascoin, *Réforme de l'Etat* (Paris, 1932), p. 37. Cf. also Hubert, *Le Principe d'autorité dans l'organisation démocratique* (Paris, 1926), p. 140; C. Guy-Grand, *L'Avenir de la démocratie* (Paris, 1928), pp. 62 ff.

democracy, as the hierarchical autonomy of the armed forces has always in the main been respected by the government, whatever the party in power. The supply services of the army and navy, however, in so far as they are under the administration of the political authorities, are very generally criticized on grounds of costliness and general inefficiency. Professor Hubert writes on this subject:

> The army must have at its disposal the enormous supplies of material required by modern warfare. The arsenals and the food warehouses must be full, the fortifications well prepared to support the army. All the auxiliary services must be well organized and all the factories mobilized. Furthermore there can be no navy without ships or with only a few out of date vessels on board of which it is still possible to die with glory but not with profit. In all these fields organization is prevision. It supposes discipline, the subordination of private interests to a general rule, an authority able to disregard the demands and lamentations of maritime hamlets, of agricultural unions, of local municipal councils, of executive committees, of labor unions, of military groups good only for parade purposes, and, above all, of electoral cliques blind to everything except the petty interests and habits of their minute constituencies.[5]

More general and more bitter still is the dissatisfaction universally expressed with the administration of the national finances. Here it is not necessary to quote any particular author. They are all equally outspoken, and the better informed and the more thoughtful they are, the more scath-

[5] *Op. cit.*, p. 149.

ing their strictures.[6] Equally unable to levy and especially to collect taxes, to reduce expenditure, and
to raise long-term loans on reasonable terms, the
French government has ever since President
Poincaré's last administration been constrained to
indulge in successive doses of inflation. The result
is that the public credit, which was before the war
one of the best established, is seriously shattered.
France, once the most important banker of the
Continent, today exports capital mainly in the
form of hot money seeking protection abroad
against monetary instability and taxation at home.

Financial policy, which was never France's
boast, under the monarchy in the eighteenth century still less than under her successive regimes in
the nineteenth, is everywhere democracy's greatest
weakness. But no contemporaneous democracy
seems more vulnerable in this respect than the
French today, and that in spite of her admirably
laborious and thrifty rural population.

We could continue almost indefinitely this tale
of woe based on the writings of French democrats,
the most severely critical comments being those on
the economic and social policies of French democracy and on the public administration in the
fields of hygiene, rural housing, public instruction,

[6] *Ibid.*, p. 135; G. Deherme, *L'immense question de l'ordre* (Paris,
1930), pp. 79 ff.; Barthélemy, *op. cit.*, 1931, p. 145; Gascoin, *op. cit.*,
pp. 32 ff., 68 ff.

and public works. Everywhere our mirror would reflect the same sad picture of dissatisfaction and of disappointment. The picture has not unnaturally become even darker in the course of the past years and months. The mad economic policies inaugurated by the *Front populaire*, which tended to enhance production by diminishing the hours of labor while increasing the rate of wages, have for obvious reasons never enriched any country. But such experiments, which the world's wealthiest commonwealth itself can afford only at its peril, are, of course, infinitely more costly when applied in France, already ruined by the war and threatened by disquieting neighbors on most of her frontiers.

The French people then—the fact may be taken as indisputable and as undisputed—are not satisfied with their democratic institutions as they are working today. To put it bluntly, they feel that they are not getting their money's worth either in security, in prosperity, in prestige, or in national dignity. The countless criticisms one hears and reads, as a rule, however, go beyond the mere recital of specific grievances. Their authors generally tend to explain these grievances, were it only in the search for means of removing them.

The reactionaries of the right, of course, do not hesitate to make democracy itself responsible for all that goes ill in their country, but they are very much embarrassed when it comes to suggesting an alternative to their present form of government. The least imaginative are content to hope for a restoration of the traditional monarchy. In their view, it is as if all would be well if only the ribbon of French destiny could be cut off in 1789 and the threads of the end of the eighteenth century sewed up with those of the beginning of the twentieth. Their rather scrappy and most unhistorical philosophy is made up of such elements as the hereditary principle, a firm but benevolently popular despotism, corporative institutions, regional decentralization, and uncompromising nationalism. Although this school of thought, if it may be so called, looks upon Italian fascism and German national-socialism with some complacency, as upon the archenemies abroad of their archenemies in France, they do not seem tempted to recommend either of these models to the imitation of their fellow-countrymen. In view of their obvious and obviously justified lack of faith in their own ability to take over the reins of power, their opinions may be disregarded as those of a sometimes picturesque but always hopelessly unconstructive opposition.

The vast body of Frenchmen realize that the era of the hereditary principle is definitely over in so far as their country is concerned, and that that of restricted suffrage, on the nature of which it would be impossible to reach agreement, has in any case not yet come. They therefore accept democracy as the inevitable basis of the state, some with unabated enthusiasm, others, probably the great majority, in a spirit of more or less reluctant resignation. Their attacks are therefore directed not against the principle of popular government itself but against its French parliamentary form. It is fair to say that in France the crisis of democracy today is essentially the crisis of French parliamentarism.

The omnipotence of an all too talkative legislature which elects an impotent head of the state, which ever more frequently overthrows ever weaker ministries, which jeopardizes by its indiscretions the independence of the judiciary, which meddles with the traditionally honest but somewhat bureaucratic civil service, which votes excessive taxes and still more excessive appropriations, but all too few well-thought-out constructive measures, and which, while obviously unable to govern and to administer itself, prevents efficient government and administration by all others—such is the general complaint.

The criticism of French parliamentarism by sincere French believers in democracy naturally raises the question of the relations between these two institutions. That there can be no democratic government without some form of elected legislature is evident both logically and historically.

EVOLUTION OF DEMOCRACY

Even the smallest and simplest political units, such as Swiss cantons and rural townships, have found it necessary to insert some legislative organ between the people and the governmental executives of their sovereign will. The French parliament, like all other legislatures, is born of this necessity.

The rights and the role of this intermediary organ vary, however, both according to constitutions and according to political habits and traditions. They vary, first, according to constitutions. In most democratic states, as in Great Britain and in France, for instance, parliament is the supreme master of the ministry which, selected according to its preferences, may continue in office only as long as it is assured of the confidence of the majority of the legislators. In other no less democratic countries, as in the United States and in Switzerland, the executive is more independent of the will of the legislature. In the United States, the president, who is both the head of the state and his own prime minister as chief of his cabinet, is elected by popular vote, while in Switzerland the Federal Council is elected by the Federal Assembly, that is, by both houses of Congress voting in common. But in the United States, as in Switzerland, the government remains in power even if its policies fail to secure the approval of a parliamentary majority. The independence of the executive is carried much farther in the United States than in Switzerland, since both the president's veto and his popular election are foreign to Swiss constitutional law. But the superiority which the American president owes to the Constitution of his country is perhaps more than compensated in favor of the Swiss Federal Council by the subserviency of the Swiss Federal Assembly, a subserviency which is a child not of its legal status but of its composition and of its parliamentary habits.

The Franco-British system, which is known as parliamentarism in the narrow sense, is by far the most widely adopted form of representative government. In practice, it presents, however, a great variety of types. Thus it seems to have yielded satisfactory results wherever the administration in power has been able to rely on a faithful parliamentary majority. That is the case, as a rule, wherever there are not more than two parties or at least solid coalitions, the stronger of which supports the government while the other constitutes the opposition.

Now the most obvious weakness of parliamentarism in France results from the multiplicity of political parties and groups. Whereas in Great Britain the government is composed of the leaders of the parliamentary majority and is therefore, as a body, endowed with all the necessary authority of leadership, in France it is made up of representatives of a variety of parties which are rarely long loyal either to their members in the government or to each other. Therefore, the French cabinet, being at the mercy of an uncertain and constantly changing parliamentary majority, is clearly the servant and not the master of the legislature.

This preponderance of the legislature, combined with its unruliness, is generally denounced as the root evil of French parliamentarism. It is responsible first for the ephemeral nature of most French ministries, of which there have been no less than thirty-six in the course of the last twenty years. Writing three years ago, Sir John Marriott recalled that "the average life of a ministry during the Third Republic has been about eight months," and adds that "there have been ninety-seven ministries since 1870."[7]

This instability of the government in its turn makes for complete irresponsibility both on the part of its individual members and on the part of the parties which support them. As no one can be called to account for the failings of the general administration and of the legislative policies of the country, very few statesmen are tempted to shape any boldly constructive measures with a view to enforcing them. They know that such measures could in no case be successfully carried out in the average lifetime of a French cabinet. As the followers will not follow, the leaders cannot and will

[7] *Dictatorship and Democracy* (Oxford, 1935), p. 164.

not lead.[8] This governmental paralysis, which is under no circumstances conducive to national prosperity and vitality, is, of course, particularly fatal in a rapidly changing world, dominated by aggressive dictators in the neighboring states. Such a world calls for resolute and consistent action on the part of the defenders of liberty. When it is lacking, we are inevitably faced with a crisis of liberty which, in France, may or may not be a crisis of democracy, but is in any case a crisis of parliamentarism.

If, having attributed this crisis to the weakness of French governments, this weakness to the restlessness and fickleness of French legislatures, and these failings to the multiplicity of French parties, we attempt to go a step farther in our analysis, we are led to inquire into the causes of this multiplicity. Why has democracy given rise in France and in other Continental countries to the division of the electorate into a dozen or more groups, none of which commands a clear popular majority, whereas elsewhere the tendency has been toward a two-party system?

The fact, which is admitted by all French students and which in other countries is sometimes as-

[8] Hubert, *op. cit.*, pp. 137 ff.; Guy-Grand, *op. cit.*, pp. 54 ff., 196 ff.; P. Archambault, *Réalisme démocratique* (Paris, 1930), pp. 30 ff.; Barthélemy, *op. cit.*, 1931, pp. 38 ff.; Gascoin, *op. cit.*, pp. 34 ff.; E. Giraud, *La Crise de la démocratie et le renforcement du pouvoir exécutif* (Paris, 1938), pp. 37 ff.

cribed to proportional representation, is not to be thus explained in France. Except for a brief experiment with proportional representation immediately after the war, France has always practiced a mode of election not dissimilar to the British. Each *député*, like each member of parliament, is elected in his own constituency, which elects only one representative. The main difference between the two systems is that whereas in Great Britain a plurality of votes is sufficient to seat, in France second ballots are held when, in the first, no candidate has obtained an absolute majority of votes. But this feature of the French system, which would seem to make for fewer and larger parties rather than the reverse, can obviously not suggest the solution of our problem. Nor can this solution be found in the fact that the French president of the Council cannot, like the British prime minister, dissolve the lower house and appeal to the electorate when threatened with defeat at the hands of an insubordinate majority.

The cause of the multiplicity of French political parties clearly lies much deeper. It has been sought for in national psychology. The individualism of the French makes the electorate averse to any form of regimentation and the elected restive under any scheme of party discipline. And the common passion for logic and theoretical consistency renders them both unwilling to accept the practical compromises necessary for collective action. The cause has been sought for also in the lack of political homogeneity which opposes Catholics and anti-clericals, Paris and the provinces, town and country, North and South, East and West, and thus constitutes an obstacle to the formation and strict discipline of large nation-wide parties.[9]

Whatever the true cause—and there are probably more than one—the fact of the inability of the French to constitute and to run a two-party system remains. This inability, which Sir John Marriott has called "the inherent vice of the parliamentary system in France,"[10] has created a crisis of democratic parliamentarism if not of democracy in the greatest of European republics.

If we cross the Channel, we are confronted with an entirely different situation. Here cabinets are stable, order is secure, the judiciary independent, the civil service efficient, public finances sound, and the people well-nigh unanimously loyal not only to the Crown but, above all, to their parliamentary institutions. And these institutions are undeniably democratic, both as the efficient instrument of the will of the British people to govern themselves and as the no less effective safeguard of the constitutional rights of the individual British subject.

[9] Cf. James Bryce, *Modern Democracies* (London, 1923), I, 297 ff.
[10] *Op. cit.*, p. 164.

Why, then, should one hear of a crisis of democracy even in the apparently happy home of democratic parliamentarism?

Before examining the British impeachment of British democracy, we must note that it is not nearly as general or as severe as is the French impeachment of French democracy. When such Englishmen as Lord Bryce, Professor Delisle Burns, Mr. M. A. Pink, Professor Harold Laski, and Sir John Marriott, not to speak of their pre-war predecessors, such as Sir Henry Maine and Mr. Lecky, write of the crisis of democracy, they draw most of their illustrations from countries other than their own. What they deplore in their studies of approximation is less the distance which separates British from ideal democracy than the remoteness of foreign imitations from their British model. However, there remains enough in their strictures which refers to British conditions to allow us to consider them briefly here without irrelevance.

In order immediately to show the change of climate experienced by the critical student of democracy when he crosses the English Channel from south to north, we will quote the following passage from a recent book, which is in many respects the most uncompromising attack on British institutions which has flowed from a British pen, or at least from a pen dipped in British ink, since the war. In his *Democracy in Crisis*, my learned and brilliant friend Professor Laski, dealing with the institutions of his country, wrote in 1933:

> It is a remarkable tradition, upon which it is difficult to dwell without complacency. The organisation of the electorate into parties; the great drama of the day-to-day struggle in Parliament, with office as the prize of victory; the opportunity afforded to able men of a splendid career built upon the proof, sternly tested in Parliament, of character and ability; the majestic and orderly progress which resulted from the effort of parties to discover national need as the path to victory; the clearcut division between them which made the confusion of coalition abhorrent to both sides; the willingness of the governing class to take the new leaders, as they arose, within the charmed circle so that *novi homines* like the Chamberlains stood upon a footing hardly less secure than that of an ancient family like the Cecils, once they had arrived; the self-confidence which could allow the amplest criticism of the system's foundations so that the most revolutionary exiles —Engels, Marx, Kropotkin—could live unhampered in its midst; the achievement of a civil service almost free from the evil of patronage, remarkably neutral, magnificently efficient, and capable of avoiding the excesses of continental bureaucracy—these are virtues which no one, regarding alternative experience, has the right to consider with any feelings save those of admiration.[11]

In spite of this eulogy on British institutions, not only its author but many other British contemporaries are sounding the death knell of British democracy. When we examine the reason of their pessimism, we discover that it is due far less to their discontent with the past and even with the present than to their apprehensions for the future.

[11] Pp. 32–33.

These disbelievers in the democracy of tomorrow may be roughly divided into two groups which, according to their estimate of the common man and their attitude toward him, may be called the right and the left.

British parliamentarism has worked well in the past, the critics of the right are likely to declare, first, because it was not truly democratic, and second, because it had to deal with relatively simple problems. It is even working tolerably well today, they add, because behind the democratic façade which is sufficiently impressive to satisfy the people by entertaining the illusion of their own sovereignty, the real power is wielded by competent but irresponsible masters. These masters the masses ignore as they ignore the masses, and they would neither seek nor obtain popular favor if they were to be thrust upon the open stage. This illusion, however, the antidemocratic critics conclude, cannot last forever. Democracy will soon be faced with a most painful dilemma. It will either have to surrender its apparent but unreal powers to those who are fit to exercise them, or, if it prefers to do away with deceptive appearances and to attempt really to run the state itself, the experiment will inevitably result in chaos. In the first case, democracy would be sacrificed to efficiency. In the second, civilization would be sacrificed to democracy. In both cases, we have a crisis of democracy.

THE CRISIS OF DEMOCRACY

Such opinions are not confined to those traditional die-hards who, in their London clubs, deplore the gradual disappearance of large estates,
who revolt against the ever increasing taxation,
who, in a word, cannot forgive democracy the in-
roads it has already made upon their former supremacy and the threats to which it exposes their
surviving privileges. These opinions are enter-
tained also in far more open-minded and disinterested quarters. We find them expounded in the
writings of such progressive intellectuals as H. G.
Wells, Aldous Huxley, and Alderton Pink.

Let us consider for a moment a recent book of the
last-named and least-known of these three authors.
In his *A Realist Looks at Democracy*, which came
out in 1930, Mr. Pink elaborates the theme that
democracy is hopelessly out of date and that it
will shortly have to make way, in Great Britain
as elsewhere, for some sort of enlightened, benevo-
lent, and humane dictatorship of the expert. Concerning the past and present of democracy, he
writes:

For generations the effective political ideas have remained
almost unchanged in the democratic states. The principles
that are now bandied about on political platforms are largely
the legacy of the eighteenth century. When first enunciated,
they were received as the inspired utterances of philosophers.
In an age of privilege and despotism the new ideas of equality
and liberty were necessary and vital. Their power overthrew
empires and re-drew the map of Europe. Those ideas, and the
ideas concerning representative government with which they

are connected, have since become sufficiently trite to be apprehended by a half-educated populace, but in a twentieth-century world they have lost their vital force. At the time of the Bourbon monarchy it was above all things necessary to assert one aspect of the truth, namely, that nobleman, priest, and peasant were equal in virtue of their common humanity; to-day it may be just as necessary to call attention to another aspect of the truth, namely, that in virtue of their natural endowments men are fundamentally unequal.[12]

Being fundamentally unequal and having to solve problems of statesmanship which under the infinitely complex conditions of modern life are bound to baffle even the greatest minds, mankind must free itself from the prejudice and from the cant of an obsolete democratic philosophy. Accordingly, Mr. Pink writes:

Democrats will need something more than the support of traditional platitudes in order to maintain their system in face of the very strong temptation to cut the Gordion knot by instituting some form of dictatorship. They will have to work out principles by which the cherished ideals of liberty, representative government, and so on, can be accommodated to the new conditions. It remains to be seen whether such a compromise is possible. On the other hand, turning from theory and the future to the facts of the present, we must take note of the obvious signs that the nineteenth-century notions concerning parliamentary institutions are losing their appeal. Not only is half Europe living under dictatorships and submitting to the abrogation of many of the elementary rights as preached by the democratic gospel, but even our own national council, the Mother of Parliaments, is losing its former prestige and has to meet dangerous challenges from direct action. These facts alone should disturb the English-

[12] P. 29.

man in his insular belief that democracy after his own pattern is the only possible form of government for a civilised nation; and if they are given their true value, they should make him re-examine the presuppositions of the democratic theory in the light of modern needs. Our fundamental requirement is to evolve a political form by which the community can take effective charge of the social and economic movements now in progress,—movements which, if not controlled, threaten the disruption of society. This can be done only by intelligent thinking. And intelligent thinking must challenge even those first principles which to a democrat are axiomatic.[13]

Intelligent thinking must be supplemented by independent action in the interests of the whole community. The present parliamentary regime, Mr. Pink holds, is conducive to neither. Success at the polls is no test of intelligence, and governmental reliance on parliamentary majorities, under our present plutocratic conditions, necessarily makes for the triumph of private interests over public welfare.

In this country we have marched stage by stage towards the ideal of representative institutions based on universal franchise. Our efforts have been in the direction of developing Parliamentary government, working on the lines of the party system. Has this machinery produced a body of legislators and administrators of anything like the kind we have demanded as necessary? Can it by any means be made to produce such a class?

Nobody, I suppose, would be prepared to maintain that the British House of Commons contains the six hundred best brains of the country, or the six hundred men who, on any but the most cynical grounds, could be adjudged the fittest to rule. . . . .[14]

[13] *Ibid.*, pp. 165–66. [14] *Ibid.*, p. 169.

.... the Government which has constantly to keep its eye on majorities is open to all kinds of unfair pressure. To-day it has to give way to the brewers; to-morrow it must pander to the bookmakers. . . . .[15]

While the voters are going through the motions of choosing whom they will for their representatives, the captains of industry and the international financiers are determining behind the scenes what persons shall be allowed to become candidates, and are organising attacks on public opinion to be carried out either by open assaults or by the subtler method of psychological penetration. And after the elections ministers and party leaders can be kept well in control by the wielders of economic power and the upholders of class privilege. The Labour Party is less amenable to these particular influences than the two older parties, but in the trade unions it has to face forces which are just as powerful, even if exerted in the opposite direction.[16]

In spite of the irrationality inherent in all democracy, Great Britain has been able to weather the storms of the nineteenth century, because during that period the realities of government are hidden behind deceptive appearances. "The voice is the voice of the people; but the hand is the hand of an oligarchy."[17]

For the future, however,

The only hope is that leaders with vision enough to see its inevitable destination will rise up to seize the controls and impose a new direction. Such leaders are not likely to be manufactured in the democratic mill, which turns out standardised articles of mediocre quality, but cannot produce the individual masterpiece stamped with genius. Modern democracy will rather discourage the right men from shouldering the public burden; and, filled with stupid complacency about

[15] *Ibid.*, p. 171.   [16] *Ibid.*, pp. 180–81.   [17] *Ibid.*, p. 179.

the right to individual judgment, it will put all sorts of ob-
stacles in the way of those who are seeking new paths.

It remains for the minority who possess real intellectual
keenness and vigour to lead the way along a fresh line of
advance, to help us to get rid of the old shibboleths, and to
discover means of replacing blundering mediocrity by pur-
poseful intelligence.[18]

We have deliberately loaded our summary of
Mr. Pink's views with quotations from his own
pen. His style and his tone show that we have to
deal not with an experienced politician or with a
learned political historian but with a brilliantly
imaginative man of letters. Obviously under the
influence of Oswald Spengler,[19] Mr. Pink can hardly be considered typical of any large body of
Englishmen of today. But his impatience of contemporary democracy and his fears for its future
in its relations with autocratic dictatorships on the
European continent are worth noting. They are
undoubtedly shared by some of the younger intellectuals who, repelled and attracted alike by the
dictatorships of Rome, Berlin, and Moscow, are
groping for a means of reconciling individual liberty with national efficiency.

We have quoted Mr. Pink as one of those whose
attacks on democracy came from the right. Re-
jecting the principle of equality, he accuses de-

[18] *Ibid.*, p. 215.

[19] *Der Untergang des Abendlandes* (2 vols.; Munich, 1927), II,
passim, and particularly pp. 577 ff.

mocracy, as a social philosophy based on this fundamental fallacy, of depriving the community of the services of the ablest of its members. Professor Laski, on the other hand, we shall summon as a witness of the left for the prosecution of democracy.

In his view, democracy, or capitalist democracy, as he prefers to call the existing regime in Great Britain, is insufficiently and not excessively egalitarian. It is not, as for Mr. Pink, true to a false ideal, but, on the contrary, false to one that is true.

Professor Laski's argument, which one finds elaborated in all his brilliant writings and particularly in his *Democracy in Crisis*, is simple in its essentials—simple and, if one admits his premises, entirely convincing. His premises are those of the thoroughgoing socialist. Capitalism in his eyes is "inherently wrong" in that it denies social equality, which is the essence of justice. Contemporary capitalism, furthermore, is practically unsuccessful in that it is more and more failing to improve the general standard of living. It is, therefore, doomed to disappear.[20]

On the other hand, it is at least doubtful whether in Great Britain capitalism can be overthrown by the normal processes of parliamentary democracy. Not only is it to be expected that a duly elected Socialist majority, "if it meant business," would find arrayed against it all the forces of tradition

[20] Laski, *op. cit.*, p. 185.

and privilege intent upon maintaining themselves, even at the cost of illegal violence, but the Socialist party itself could not rely solely on the principles of political democracy to retain power and to protect its accomplishments against a possible legal and parliamentary counteroffensive of capitalism. Therefore, democracy is in crisis. This crisis results from an internal conflict between true democracy, which for Professor Laski is synonymous with egalitarian socialism, and capitalist democracy, which favors the maintenance of the prevailing regime with its undemocratic inequalities. This thought is nowhere more clearly expressed than in the following passage:

The discipline of capitalist democracy is in decay because the principle of capitalism cannot be squared with the principle of democracy. The one consistently seeks to maintain inequalities which the other, not less consistently, seeks to abolish.[21]

The most significant statement in Professor Laski's recent book is, however, that in which he clearly repudiates parliamentary democracy if it is to constitute an obstacle to the advent of socialism. He is a sincere democrat himself and he handsomely recognizes the great achievements of British parliamentarism in the course of the nineteenth century. But he is above all a Socialist, and if parliamentary democracy and socialism should come into conflict, he would sacrifice democracy to

[21] *Ibid.*, p. 215.

socialism, just as he expects that capitalistic democrats would, in their turn, sacrifice democracy to
capitalism, if capitalism could not otherwise be
saved.

The passage in question is the following:

> I believe, therefore, that the attainment of power by the
> Labour Party in the normal electoral fashion must result in a
> radical transformation of parliamentary government. Such
> an administration could not, if it sought to be effective, ac-
> cept the present forms of its procedure. It would have to
> take vast powers, and legislate under them by ordinance and
> decree; it would have to suspend the classic formulae of normal
> opposition. If its policy met with peaceful acceptance, the
> continuance of parliamentary government would depend upon
> its possession of guarantees from the Conservative Party that
> its work of transformation would not be disrupted by repeal
> in the event of its defeat at the polls. Could such guarantees
> be given? Would they be implemented if they were? I do
> not know. I suggest that their exaction is inevitable as part
> of the price of peace when such great issues are in dispute.
> And it is obvious that the natural history of a legislative as-
> sembly under such conditions would be quite different from
> anything we have previously known.[22]

Professor Laski's analysis of the reasons why
British parliamentary democracy worked satis-
factorily throughout the nineteenth century is extremely enlightening. He attributes its admitted
success primarily to the fact that the two parties
which dominated the House of Commons and
faithfully represented the public opinion of the nation were in constant agreement on all essentials

[22] *Ibid.*, p. 87.

and differed only in minutiae. Both parties, he writes, "were in substantial agreement upon the vital importance of liberal individualism, especially in the industrial realm; both refused to see the state as more than a supplementary corrective of the more startling deficiencies of individual execution."[23]

Furthermore, he shows how the legislative problems which called for solution were relatively simple in a time of continuous and remarkable economic expansion. No less enlightening is his analysis of the difficulties with which political democracy is confronted today, even in Great Britain. A new party has arisen which challenges not only this or that feature of the existing regime but its very basis, and this at a time when the business of government has become infinitely more exacting, more complicated, and more technical.

All this will be readily admitted by the thoughtful and impartial friend of democracy. When, however, Professor Laski proceeds to declare that British democracy is in crisis also because it may well prove unable to effect and to protect radical reforms which may not be demanded by a majority at the polls with sufficient insistence or supported with sufficient persistence to secure their permanency, then he is clearly passing from the democratic to the dictatorial camp. It is as if—to make

[23] *Ibid.*, p. 34.

our point clear with deliberate exaggeration but not, we believe, with any unfairness—a French royalist or a British republican were to denounce democracy as unable to restore monarchy in France or to abolish it in Great Britain in the face of popular opposition or, at least, in the absence of sufficient popular support. In such a case, one might properly speak of the crisis of royalism in France and of republicanism in Great Britain, but not of the crisis of democracy in either country. Likewise, if the British Labor party should find itself unable or unwilling to persuade the majority of the British electorate of the wisdom of doing away permanently with capitalism in favor of communism, the result might be a crisis of radical socialism, but not of democracy, in Great Britain.

Such British indictments as those of Mr. Pink and of Professor Laski remain exceptional however. They should not blind us to the obvious fact that in Great Britain, much more than in France and at least as much as in any other of the surviving democracies, popular government remains the preference and commands the loyalty of the overwhelming majority of the community. Even the two authors we have quoted would doubtless admit that the crisis of democracy was not a specifically British phenomenon, but one which was discussed in Great Britain mainly because it was noticeable elsewhere.

THE CRISIS OF DEMOCRACY

To consider but one more of the surviving democracies of Europe, let us turn for a brief moment to Switzerland. Here, as in Great Britain and in France, democratic institutions were set up and consolidated in the course of the nineteenth century. In view of the historical traditions of the country, of its small size, and of its subdivision into over a score of self-governing cantons, democracy was even carried farther than anywhere else, except that the fair sex were not admitted, or rather obliged, to share in its operations. Here also, as in Great Britain and in France, the increasing complexity of economic life and the will of democracy itself have burdened the state with ever heavier responsibilities. Here also, therefore, democracy has been confronted with problems of popular control such as were never dreamed of by its founders. Here also, as in France but not in Great Britain, the electorate has been split up into a multiplicity of political parties, none of which today commands a clear majority in the national legislature. Here also, as in Great Britain and in France, democracy underwent a self-willed eclipse during the war, when all legislative powers were concentrated in the hands of the executive. Here, more than in either Great Britain or France, the constitutional rights of the people have since remained somewhat curtailed, under the pressure of

internal and external circumstances. Here also,
finally, although much less than in France and
no more than in Great Britain, the crisis of democracy has become a topic of current discussion.

Let us consider the relevant facts somewhat
more closely. When modern democracy was established in Switzerland by the federal constitution of 1848, the dominant social creed was that of
economic no less than of political liberalism. Pro-
tective tariffs, government subsidies, and all other
forms of state intervention in favor of particular
private, professional, or local interests were condemned as severely as all special privileges, all
limitations on personal liberty, and all restrictions
on universal suffrage.

Little by little, however, as democracy had subjected the state to the will of the individual, the
individual sought to use the state for the promotion
of his material ends. In 1874, the constitution of
1848 was amended in order to make it still more
completely democratic by the introduction of the
legislative referendum. At the same time, however, the federal state was strengthened at the expense of the cantons and invited to play a more
active part in the defense of the social and economic interests of its citizens. From 1874 until the
present day, economic liberalism has been gradu-

ally discarded in favor of increasingly ambitious policies of state intervention.[24]

This has not unnaturally led to a change in the character and to an increase in the number of political parties. Before 1874, the electorate was divided into two principal groups, Liberal-Radical and Conservative, according to their views on purely constitutional issues such as federalism, clericalism, democratic rights, etc. As the federal government came to adopt policies which were calculated to exercise an immediate influence on the material welfare of the various classes of the population, new parties were founded to represent these necessarily conflicting interests. Thus the Radical party became completely divorced from the Liberal, and to them and to the surviving Conservative party were added first the Socialists, then an Agrarian party, then a Communist group, and finally, in 1935, a Consumers' party and a so-called Young Peasant group.

The system of proportional representation for congressional elections to the lower house, which was introduced in 1918, naturally favored this splitting-up of the electorate into small groups, which had already begun as a consequence of the abandonment of economic liberalism. According-

[24] A detailed study of this evolution is to be found in the author's *L'Individu et l'Etat*, pp. 270 ff., and a summary of its principal phases in his *Government of Switzerland*, pp. 107 ff.

ly, there are today eight parties represented in the federal parliament, not one of which can count on even a third of the votes of the legislature.

The result of this has been that the federal executive, which from 1848 until 1891 was composed entirely of Radical-Liberals, was obliged to admit first one and then two Conservative members and recently a representative of the Agrarian group. This has, of course, made for less clear-cut and consistent policies and for a general method of government by bargaining and by compromise, which has not enhanced the prestige of democracy.

During the World War, as we have seen, the federal government was granted full powers and the federal state became the almighty arbiter and indeed the unquestioned master of all private interests. Although with the return of peace a reaction set in, it has succeeded neither in restoring to parliament the full measure of the influence it formerly enjoyed nor in freeing private enterprise from the grip of state control.

It is obvious that these changes in the structure and in the policies of the federal government have had their repercussions on the processes if not on the temper of Swiss democracy. The direct influence of the people on the course of legislation has been doubly weakened thereby. On the one hand, the legislative issues have become so involved that they are no longer readily understood, and, on the other, the executive and the legislature, having once reached a compromise on a given measure, are more and more reluctant to expose it to the veto of the electorate.

According to the federal constitution, "all federal laws are submitted to the approval or rejection of the people, if 30,000 qualified voters or eight cantons demand that they shall be." But, as the constitution also provides that "the same rule applies to federal ordinances when they are of general *and not of an urgent character*," it has left open a loophole through which much legislation has passed without being submitted to the referendum in the course of the last years. The Federal Council has recently admitted that from 1931 until April 1, 1938, eighty federal ordinances adopted by the legislature have been declared urgent and thus withdrawn from the judgment of the people at the polls.[25]

This antidemocratic practice has called forth a sharp popular protest. There are at present under consideration two constitutional amendments put forward on initiative petitions, tending to limit the use of the emergency clause and thus to restore to the electorate a fundamental right of which they have been unconstitutionally deprived. Everyone in Switzerland feels that the present

[25] *Rapport du Conseil fédéral à l'Assemblée fédérale sur l'initiative tendant à restreindre l'emploi de la clause d'urgence du 10 mai 1938*, p. 6.

position is unsatisfactory. There is no doubt that the emergency clause has been abused by the government in connivance with the parliamentary majority. On the other hand, there is also a widespread conviction that this abuse was, if not entirely unavoidable, at least largely justified by the dangers to which a demagogic use of the referendum might have exposed the country in several critical junctures.

In so far, one may well speak of a crisis of democracy or at least of direct democracy in Switzerland. But it is really a case of democracy distrusting itself and not of its being challenged from without. In times of real internal difficulties or external perils, the majority of the popularly elected legislature and the government of their own free choice have in the case of certain measures, notably in the field of taxation, of which they knew that they were unpopular but felt that they were necessary, unconstitutionally agreed to avoid the danger of being disavowed at the polls.

As the members of the legislature have, however, been constantly assured of the continued confidence of their voters at subsequent elections of which no one can question the absolute freedom and sincerity, it would be absurd to accuse anyone of dictatorial ambitions in this connection. That there has been a tendency temporarily to deprive the individual citizen of the exercise of certain of his constitutional rights is undeniable. But that this tendency might lead to the permanent denial of these rights is, to say the least, most unlikely.

If the captain of an airship should, without being legally empowered thereto, forbid smoking on board, the passengers would probably grumble and one or the other might even revolt. But if they felt that the prohibition, although illegal, was not inherently unreasonable and was dictated not by any selfish caprice but by considerations of general security, they would submit. If they should, furthermore, of their own free will take passage under the same captain for their return trip, it would hardly be fair for them, on their safe arrival, to accuse him of unjustified dictatorial dispositions. The community would be well advised, however, expressly to endow the captain with the rights which he had hitherto wisely but illegally exercised.

Such, roughly, is the political position in Switzerland today. While opposing the constitutional changes proposed by the above-mentioned initiative petitions, the Federal Council is itself advocating an amendment to the fundamental law. It recommends that the following clause be substituted for the provision at present in force:

Federal ordinances of general importance, which must be enforced without delay, may be declared urgent with the consent of one half at least of all the members of each house. If they are so declared they may not be submitted to the vote of the people. The validity of urgent federal ordinances must be limited in time.[26]

Other symptoms, if not of a crisis of Swiss democracy, at least of reactions against the entirely liberal democracy prevailing in Switzerland before the World War are to be found in the anticommunistic legislation adopted by the majority of the people in several cantons recently and in the more rigidly enforced limitations of the freedom of the press and of assembly in matters of foreign policy.

These measures have naturally aroused the indignation of those against whom they were directed and of their liberal sympathizers.[27] It seems difficult, however, to subscribe to such statements as those made recently by a Zurich lawyer to the effect that such measures "represent not only an overthrow of the political régime of Switzerland but even a danger for its national existence.[28] When one recalls that these and similar utterances were made at a conference which was summoned under Communist auspices, one cannot but feel some surprise at the lack of sense of proportion which they display. If any malcontent in the

[26] *Ibid.*, p. 21.

[27] Cf. for instance the indictments of these tendencies in *Régression des principes de liberté dans les réformes constitutionnelles de certains États démocratiques* (Paris: Assoc. Jurid. Internat., 1938), pp. 74 ff., 114 ff.

[28] *Ibid.*, p. 100.

Soviet Union were rash enough to express his dissatisfaction with prevailing conditions with only one-tenth of the violence that is every day resorted to, with entire impunity, by the Swiss press of the extreme left, he would immediately pay for his folly with his personal liberty, if not with his life.

It would therefore be well to maintain some sense of equity and to remember that all the freedom of thought and of speech still enjoyed by our generation has become the monopoly of the surviving democracies, of which Switzerland is still one of the most liberal.

This should not, however, blind us to the fact that the temper not only of the government but also of the people of Switzerland is less tolerant today than it was a generation ago, that intolerance is likely to breed violence and to promote arbitrariness, and that therefore democracy must be protected by the vigilance of its friends in Switzerland as elsewhere.

However, placed as she is between two dictatorships and a democratic neighbor in which a lack of civic discipline is daily imperiling the existence of democracy, Switzerland may be excused for what lapses from political freedom she is accused of in some quarters, Swiss and foreign, today. The impartial historian of the future will certainly recognize that in these troubled post-war and, who knows, pre-war days, the best servants of democ-

racy were not those who pleaded for unlimited individual license at any cost, but those who sought
to defend political liberty by so defining it as to
enable it to defend itself.

As we see it, democracy in Switzerland is not
really threatened by the above-mentioned restrictive measures but rather by two other dangers.
These dangers we see, on the one hand, in the lack
of political leadership which characterizes the present position and, on the other, in the economic and
financial policies which are being pursued and
which, if carried much farther, might well ruin democracy by crushing it under intolerable burdens.

The first of these dangers, which has suggested
the title of a recent little book, *A People Without
Guidance*,[29] is due primarily to the perhaps accidental lack of any strong and inspiring personalities among the present rulers of the country. But
it may well be due also to a parliamentary situation in which strong and inspiring leadership has
become difficult if not impossible. When a government can maintain itself in power only by placat-
ing rival social groups, by economic and financial
concessions at the expense of the general interest,
the immediate demand is less for forceful than for
clever, agile, and supple leadership. Switzerland
has long been fortunate in the intelligence and in
the integrity of her political chiefs. But her form

[29] Alfred Amrein, *Volk ohne Führung* (Zurich, 1937).

of collective anonymous administration has never favored the emergence of outstanding personalities, and her present policies are particularly unpropitious in this respect.

As for these policies, they in themselves, in our view, constitute the second and major danger threatening democracy in Switzerland, as elsewhere. We shall therefore have occasion to revert to them in our next and final chapter, in which we propose to consider the general future of popular government.

CHAPTER VI

THE FUTURE OF DEMOCRACY

Nothing is more interesting and nothing is less scientific than speculations about the political future. The work of a student who seeks to recall and to analyze the past may or may not be scientific. Or rather, it is more or less scientific according to his ability to discover, select, and explain significant facts, irrespective of his personal likes and dislikes, hopes and fears, wishes and repugnances. The best history is that which, having been written before the event, would have been most accurately confirmed by what really took place later.

Now, writing after the event, it is difficult enough to ascertain the facts, more difficult still to select the most significant, that is, those whose influence was greatest on the immediate and on the distant future, and, most difficult of all, to explain them properly, that is, to ascribe them to the factors to whose operation they really owed their emergence. In all these processes the occasions for error, misstatement, and misjudgment are so innumerable, that it would be a bold or a blind historian who would claim absolute scientific certainty for his assertions. He would be no historian at all, however, if his quest was merely for the entertainment of his readers or for the satisfaction of his personal prejudices and not primarily for truth.

But, if it is not always easy to escape the grip of personal bias and never possible to discover the whole truth, even when one is discussing the past, it is obviously out of the question in considering the future. In the unknown and unknowable future there is no truth to discover and therefore no occasion for the exercise of scientific activity.

And still, whenever a historian ventures to prolong beyond today the lines of an evolution he has sought to trace from the distant past up to the immediate present, he is assured of a far wider hearing than when he is content to remain within the bounds of his own sphere. Nor is this at all surprising. The knowledge and understanding of the past satisfy only the curiosity of the critical mind, which, in our benighted mankind, is limited to a narrow circle. Speculation about the future, on the other hand, both appeals to the imagination, which is the gift of the many, and touches upon vital interests, which are the concern of all.

It is not my purpose in submitting these remarks to deny the value of the scientific study of history for an intelligent consideration of the problems of tomorrow. These preliminary observations are intended solely to warn the inadvertent reader that we are about to abandon one form of mental exercise for another. We are now leaving the firm ground of reality, about which our statements may or may not have been true but always will remain subject to critical revision, to take our flight into the air of incalculable possibilities. What we submit from now on cannot be either true or untrue today, but only more or less reasonable in its conjectures about tomorrow. It is not even possible to assert that the most reasonable surmise is necessarily the most likely to come true. A reasonable surmise about the political future is one based on an accurate knowledge of past facts, on a fair estimate of their present significance, and on the assumption that men will continue to behave as they have been known to behave in history. Now, as this assumption may well prove fallacious in these times of feverish mysticism and of unpredictable panic, that which may reasonably be expected and which therefore seems plausible today may prove completely untrue tomorrow. Looking back over the last twenty years, no one will deny that it is very often the unlikely which has happened. It is therefore quite possible that it is again the unlikely that will happen in the course of the next decades— quite possible and, we may add, devoutly to be hoped, for it must be admitted that the prospects which seem most likely today are certainly not the most reassuring for tomorrow.

THE CRISIS OF DEMOCRACY

In considering the future of democracy, primarily in Europe, two distinct questions naturally arise: Will democracy reconquer the states now under dictatorships? Will dictatorship spread over the surviving democracies?

Before attempting to reply to these two questions in turn, let us formulate the following five general propositions concerning the past, which may perhaps throw some light on the probable future.

1. All the dictatorships prevailing in Europe, and indeed in the world today, have been set up in countries in which democracy had either been unknown or had at least never firmly taken root and had never flourished before. Therefore, it cannot be claimed that dictatorship has as yet anywhere clearly triumphed over true democracy. What it has triumphed over has been revolutionary disorder, royal absolutism or quasi-absolutism, and quasi-democratic regimes set up under constitutions hastily fashioned after foreign patterns and ill adapted to the social structure and historical traditions of the nations concerned.

2. No new dictatorship has ever been welcomed by a prosperous and contented people. Whether we look to Russia, to Italy, to Germany, to Austria, to the Baltic or to the Succession states, to South America or to Japan, always and everywhere it was poverty, misery, humiliation, and unemployment which have plowed up the social

soil in which the seeds of dictatorship have germi-
nated. It does not follow either that all democratic nations are prosperous and contented or that
all dictatorially governed nations are condemned
to permanent poverty and dissatisfaction. However, it does seem to be a significant fact that favorable economic conditions do not make for the rise
of dictatorships.

3. A third well-established fact seems to be that
the prevailing dictatorial regimes are almost all, if
not all, the offspring of the World War. In some
cases, as in Russia and in Hungary, the filiation
was immediate and direct. But in most of the
others, and particularly in Italy and in Germany,
the timelag separating the conclusion of peace and
the establishment of autocratic rule should not
prevent any impartial historian from stressing the
causal relations between the latter and the general
and individual consequences of the great struggle.
Again it does not follow that all major wars sooner
or later lead all belligerents to submit to a dictatorship or that dictatorships would be inconceivable
except as a result of international conflicts. But
the methods of authority and the habits of blind
obedience which war always promotes among gov-
erners and governed, respectively, are bound to
favor the rise of dictatorships as they undeniably
tend to undermine the foundations of political
liberty.

4. Democracy, which was on the winning side during the World War, has survived only among the victors and among the neutrals who, in some respects, were more victorious than those even who imposed their terms on their defeated enemies. Again we do not claim that either all the victors or all the neutrals were and are democratic. The cases of Italy, Japan, and Spain would suffice to belie such an allegation. But we cannot fail to be impressed by the coincidence between the survival of democracy in France, Belgium, Great Britain, the British Dominions, the United States, Holland, the Scandinavian states, and Switzerland, and the absence of any of the defeated powers from this list.

5. Finally, there is another coincidence which is so general as to seem still less fortuitous. It is that between the creditor states and the democracies in the world today. Not only are none of the great debtor nations to be found among the democracies, but there are no creditor nations among those governed by dictatorships. To be sure, this does not imply that their democracy is the factor which allows some nations to lend more than they borrow, or, especially, that a conversion to democracy suffices to turn the balance of accounts in favor of the neophyte. It would indeed seem more reasonable to reverse the proposition. It is probably not so much because some states are democracies that

they are in a position to lend, as because other states are obliged to borrow, that they are not democracies. However, whether we look upon dictatorship as the regime best adapted to the needs of the "have-not" or "proletarian" countries or whether we point to their lavish expenditure for military and other public works as one of the circumstances which prevents them from paying their debts abroad, the coincidence is both undeniable and significant.

Let us now, in the light of these propositions and other directly relevant considerations, inquire into the probable future of the dictatorships.

That the present dictators hold an appreciable number of trump cards and that they are, as a rule, playing their hand with remarkable skill should be obvious to their foes no less than to their friends. The first of these trumps is their complete and unquestioned control over all the armed forces in their respective countries. In the present highly industrialized state of the production and use of arms and ammunitions and with the available methods of communication and transport by air, overland and by sea, revolutions, insurrections, and even individual acts of violence have become well-nigh impossible. As long as a modern dictator is sure of the obedience of the army, the navy, the air force, and the police, his internal position is bound to be secure, whatever his degree of popularity with the civilian population.

That is why, although with the exception of Marshal Pilsudski of Poland, the European dictators have not been military commanders, their supreme ambition has always been to secure for themselves the undivided loyalty of all the armed forces of the nation. And in this effort they have, it would seem, been generally successful. It is in itself not difficult to understand why an energetic and nationalistic dictator should easily find favor in military circles, in which parliament and parliamentary governments are traditionally disliked. Moreover, especially in Germany, where the struggle against forced disarmament was one of the fundamental articles in the National-Socialist creed, the dictators have always sought to gain the good graces of the army. In this also they have succeeded. By increasing the effectives and the efficiency of the forces, by providing for the rapid promotion of the officers most friendly to their regime, and by improving the lot of the soldiers, they have come to be more or less willingly accepted as their supreme commander. In this effort they have not even feared to offend their closest followers, between whom and the army a rivalry dangerous for them has sometimes seemed to threaten their position.

The second trump in the dictators' game is their complete control of the means of influencing public opinion. From the kindergarten to the university, from the pamphlet to the pseudo-scientific encyclopedia, from the moving-picture show to the organization of sports, from the private conversation to the public speech addressed to hundreds of thousands and heard over the radio by millions, all possible means are employed to create a mass opinion in favor of the dictators and their regime, which they seek to identify with the national interest. If this effort, which strikes at the roots of true democracy much more menacingly than coercion by violence, were fully successful, the use of physical force would of course become unnecessary. That it is not fully successful is shown by the importance which the dictators continue to attach to the latter.

In Germany, as well as in Italy, the immediate effect of state-organized mass propaganda seems to have been to create a certain superficial and vociferous unanimity but, at the same time, to breed a profound skepticism in the people. Realizing, in spite of the collective suggestion to which they are exposed from morning to night and from birth to death, that censorship, the exclusion of foreign news, and the proclamation of official verities would all be superfluous if there were no truths to be hidden and no errors to be propagated, they appear to have a deep-seated feeling that they are being misled. What they cannot know exactly is why and in how far they are being misled. Therefore, although their critical sense is inevitably dulled by the absence of all contradiction and of all organized opposition, their feelings toward a regime which can arouse delirious enthusiasm by the eloquence of its leaders and by its impressive pageantry, but not complete confidence in its veracity, are bound to be uncertain. As long as all goes well, this may be without serious disadvantages. But how a people accustomed, even in times of success, to disbelieve its chiefs would react under the stress of disaster and calamity may be imagined but not foretold with assurance.

The boisterous, hectic, and uninterruptedly provocative tone of the speeches one hears over the radio from Berlin and from Rome does not seem to indicate that the confidence which is proclaimed with such noisy, nervous reiteration is really felt either by the orators themselves or by their shrieking audiences. It is as if all misgivings were being constantly shouted down without being psychologically silenced either in the souls of the haranguing leaders or in those of their wildly cheering followers. However, foreign opinion on this important point can be but conjectural. In speaking with Germans and Italians, one sometimes wonders whether they really know themselves what their true convictions are, so great is the domination of their aroused instincts over their critical consciousness.

What would seem less uncertain, however, is that in the long run the denial of all liberty of information, of thought, of speech, and of controversy can but affect unfortunately the mind, the intellectual resiliency, and the creative inventiveness of a people. It is relatively easy when one enjoys the undisputed mastery of all the material and external means of social control to prevent a nation from thinking freely and constructively. What is more difficult is to make it so think—much more difficult, but also much more important for its future.

A third trump card of the dictators is the opinion they have inspired of their own strenuous ability, of their energy, of their individual disinterestedness, if one may so call their ambitious devotion to the greatness of their country, and of their apparent freedom from all forms of common self-indulgence. The dictators, and in particular Signor Mussolini and Herr Hitler, have not unsuccessfully sought to strike the imagination of their people as great men, not only because they accomplish great things, but because their virtues place them above the level of their fellow-countrymen. None of the contemporary dictators seems to resemble the tyrants of old, either in their voluptuous indolence or in their self-seeking rapacity or in their tendency to sacrifice the general interest to their personal, as distinct from their nationalistic, ends.

If they display a shocking indifference to the rights of their rivals as well as to the sufferings of their victims, if they show none of the chivalrous generosity toward their enemies which is inseparable from true greatness, if they lack humanity and preach a doctrine of hardness, they practice it on themselves no less than on others.

It is true that they have until now constantly had to struggle for their popularity and have as yet had no time to succumb to the more obvious dangers of omnipotence. Still, the example of their untiring energy, of their virile love of responsibility, and of their personal courage has undoubtedly inspired their nations, or at least the younger generations thereof, and has engendered a form of hero-worship which is surely a true asset for their regimes.

Finally, their major trump has of course been the success they have heretofore achieved both in their internal and in their foreign policy.

However severely one may judge the ruthless brutality of their methods, Signor Mussolini and Herr Hitler have been uncommonly efficient administrators of their respective states. They have endowed their countries, which they found depressed and impoverished on their advent to power, with a material equipment for which some of their wealthier neighbors may well envy them. They have done away with unemployment and sloth as no democracy has as yet succeeded in doing. They have improved public health and even, if one may believe their vital statistics, increased the birth-rate. By all these and similar other achievements they have raised the spirit of their nations, which in Italy before 1922 as in Germany before 1933, was that of revolted, disunited, and demoralized peoples.

The cost, it is true, has been stupendous. The general standard of living, when measured by the volume of consumable goods earned by the common man, seems to have fallen rather than risen. But social discontent and unrest are certainly less evident and probably less real than at their accession to power. The burden of taxation and of public indebtedness has become crushing. But as it has been made to bear on the wealthy still more than on the poor, and as the volume of production has at least been maintained, Italy and Germany seem both to be standing the strain with remarkable fortitude or at least resignation.

All signs point to the fact that the introduction of dictatorships in Italy and in Germany has led to an appreciable gain in the yield of the economic effort imposed on the two nations. The reduction of unemployment, the suppression of all stoppage of work formerly due to labor troubles, and the authoritarian methods employed to mobilize and to distribute public credit and to speed up production have allowed these two countries, poor in natural resources but blessed by extremely laborious populations, to hold their own in international competition.

They have done so, in Germany and to a less extent in Italy at the expense of their foreign creditors, in spite of military and other unproductive expenditure which has reached tremendous proportions. While depriving their people of the immediate benefit of the exceptional efforts demanded of them, they have undoubtedly enhanced their prestige and their influence in the sphere of world power politics. The economic life has been subjected to a regime comparable to that prevailing in military barracks, a regime of authority, of discipline, of strenuous work, and of cheap pay. Both countries, with all their resources, natural and human, have been placed at the service of the state and the state at the service of the nationalistic ambitions of their leaders.

In the field of foreign politics, the results, when judged by the standards of their authors, have not been less impressive and remarkable. Italy has won a war against an enemy who was obviously no worthy rival and no match for her perfectly equipped troops, but who had been victorious over the armies of pre-war Italy at the end of the nineteenth century. By her victory, Italy, having annexed a large and potentially valuable part of Afri-

THE FUTURE OF DEMOCRACY

ca, has created a colonial empire of which she has forced recognition on an indignantly reluctant world. She has successfully defied the League of Nations and, with the United States in 1919, Japan in 1931, and Germany in 1933, has been the chief factor of its present impotency. By her military power and her aggressive foreign policies she has succeeded in forging the Rome-Berlin axis, which is today a major element in the diplomatic situation on the continent of Europe.

The international record of National-Socialist Germany is perhaps still more startling. Of a disarmed and isolated state the Führer has in the brief space of half a decade made the Third Reich of today. Having bullied all its neighbors into submission, alliance, or passive resignation, it clearly dominates central Europe and speaks in the tone of at least an equal to its terrified Franco-British victors of twenty years ago.

In fact, since the recent incorporation of Austria into the German Empire, it can without paradox or exaggeration be said to have won rather than lost the World War. Certainly the accretion of territory and population, which the developments of the last twenty-five years have brought Germany, far outweighs her losses incurred during the same period. She is today more powerful and more threatening to her neighbors than she was in 1914.

Thus the political achievements of the Italian

and of the German dictators in the foreign as in the internal fields have been no less than colossal, always of course judged by their own standards. Whether these achievements are as beneficial for the future of civilization as they are momentarily impressive, is of course an entirely different question and one to which the reply will depend primarily upon one's sense of social and moral values. Whether these achievements are likely to be as lasting as they have been sudden, is yet another entirely different question.

All peoples are not alike today, and in the course of history they have all been known to change their temperament and their tastes. However, with various degrees of constancy and intensity, all peoples prefer order to disorder, regular work to unemployment and insecurity, national satisfactions to national humiliations. In these respects, the Italian and the German peoples have reason to be content with their dictators.

On the other hand, all peoples prefer liberty to oppression, mutual confidence and friendliness to constant intimidation, peace to war. In these respects, the subjects of all dictatorships, of the Russian no less than of the Italian and of the German, have every reason to sigh for a change.

The future of every dictatorship will to a large extent depend on the balance between the satisfaction and the weariness, the discontent and the revolt their policies will have bred in their peoples and particularly among the younger generation. How do matters stand today in the existing dictatorships? What would be the result of an absolutely free, secret, and therefore sincere popular vote in Italy, Germany, and elsewhere, if the question were put: "Do you wish to retain or to repudiate your present form of government?" The result would, of course, to a large degree depend upon the alternative regime the people might be led to expect. And this in turn would largely depend upon the state of mind prevailing in the neighboring democracies as seen from the dictatorships. If, in the opinion of the dictatorially ruled peoples their democratic neighbors were tolerably well satisfied with their lot, the former would probably wish for a change. If not, the chances are that they would prefer to remain in their present state.

What the outcome of such a vote would be, no one can predict. The views one may gather in private conversation on the subject with sons and daughters of dictatorships are conflicting and clearly reflect individual preferences rather than rational forecasts. Even if the replies were overwhelmingly against the maintenance of the existing dictatorships, it would not, of course, follow that a revolution was imminent, because unpopular but ambitious autocrats may today better even than in the past defend themselves against their peoples as long as they can count on the obedience of their armed followers.

One thing is certain. None of the present dictators have ever felt inclined to take a chance with a sincere referendum on the loyalty of their peoples. Not only have they never organized any elections in which the voters were even technically free to express their preferences through the ballot box, but also they are always exerting all their efforts, which are ruthlessly energetic, and devoting all their skill, which is remarkable, to prevent their peoples from forming an independent judgment and from obtaining frank and impartial information from either within or without their own countries.

The ostentatious but most unspontaneous popular demonstrations intended to display the might of the dictators and the enthusiastic loyalty of their followers of course prove nothing whatever—except the ability of their organizers and the well-disciplined docility of the organized. The very fear of political freedom which characterizes all dictatorial regimes may spring from many motives. But that it is not born of complete confidence in their own popularity must occur even to themselves and to their peoples, as it is obvious to all the outside world. Whereas every election in a truly democratic state is in reality a plebiscite on democracy, a free vote on dictatorship is perhaps the only form of dictatorial propaganda to which no dictator has ever dreamed of resorting. But, of all the means of impressing the opinion of their more liberal contemporaries, it would be the only truly convincing one.

Far more significant than anything that has ever happened or has ever been caused to happen within any of the existing dictatorships as a means of testing their real popularity and therefore of assessing their probable future are events such as the plebiscite of the Saar and the popular manifestations in Danzig and in the German-speaking districts of Czechoslovakia. Here we have to deal with people who had every means of forming an independent judgment on the relative value of democracy and of Nazi dictatorship and who seem deliberately to prefer the latter.

Even these tests, however, are by no means fully convincing. It is not so much that the populations in question were and are all subjected to intensive Nazi propaganda and intimidation, that weakens the case for dictatorship that may be made out of their example. Had they been and were they so inclined, they might well have resented both. They had free access to all relevant information and also to actual support from other sources. What weakens the case is that the choice they had or have before them was or is not a dictatorship or a democracy of their own choice, but a dictatorship of their own race or a foreign democracy.

What the people of the Saar, of Danzig, of Austria, and of the Sudeten countries have shown the world is that there is, among those Germans who feel that they ought to belong to the German Reich, no insuperable repugnance against Hitlerism. When we compare their feelings with those of my German or Italian Swiss fellow-countrymen, who today less than ever feel attracted toward Nazi Germany and Fascist Italy, we may realize the importance of such historical affiliations.

When considering the probable future of the existing dictatorships, two further considerations should be borne in mind.

First, their regime was established at a time of profound political and economic depression, and it has developed under generally improving conditions. That these conditions of enhanced national prestige, increased production, and reduced unemployment, cannot continue to improve forever, is obvious. Were it only for their geographical propinquity and rival designs on the Balkans, Germany and Italy cannot both indefinitely continue their course of diplomatic victories. And in the economic field, history, which has never known a period of continuous progress and expansion, is not likely to change its course just to suit the existing dictators.

THE FUTURE OF DEMOCRACY

What will happen when reverses and disappointments set in, as they sooner or later inevitably must, is the supreme question for the future of their regimes. As long as their peoples feel engaged in a hard but victorious struggle under their leadership, their power is not likely to be shaken. But, as they have claimed even more than their full measure of credit for all the successes achieved by their nations up to date, they will have to bear more than their full measure of responsibility and of discredit for their future reverses.

Another circumstance which prevents one from believing in the permanency of the present dictatorial regimes is their highly personal character. This would seem to be most prominent in the case of Italy, where Mussolini's policy has obviously been to tolerate no striking personalities and therefore no possible rivals in his immediate surroundings. In spite of the National-Socialist insistence on the *Führerprinzip*, it would seem to be somewhat less so in Germany. Although one more often speaks of Hitlerism than of Mussolinism, there is no doubt that the Führer has shown more confidence in his immediate associates and more generosity toward them than has the Duce. As for Soviet Russia, where Stalin has apparently succeeded in securing for himself a position of solitary omnipotence unequaled even by Lenin, such a position is clearly less called for and less justified by the prevailing social philosophy than in either Italy or Germany.

As it is impossible to assess the relative importance of coercive force and of sincere hero-worship as factors of dictatorial authority in any of the existing dictatorships, it is obviously futile to seek to establish any certain comparisons between them in this respect. In view of the recent hecatombs of leading Communists in Russia, it would seem as if the ruling Comrade deemed himself less assured of the personal loyalty of his followers than either the Duce or the Führer. The latter, since the bloody suppression of the Roehm plot in 1934, has reserved his furies for his enemies and allowed his friends more fully to share with him the responsibilities of supreme power than either his Russian or his Italian colleague.

However, in all the dictatorships, the personality of the chief is, of course, and in fact, by definition, a far more important condition of political stability than in governments by the free consent of the governed. Now these chiefs are not immortal. In view of the professional risks of their trade, they would even seem to be less so than the average man.

In speculating about the permanency of their regimes, one is therefore naturally led to inquire into the probable consequences of their disappearance from the earthly scene. Can the transmission of power from the founders and undisputed heads of these regimes to their successors be effected without weakening or even overthrowing them? These successors can obviously not appeal either to the hereditary principle as in monarchies or aristocracies,[1] or to that of the freely expressed popular will as in democracies. Even if the deceased dictator had by testament decided on and proclaimed the name of his successor, would his posthumous authority suffice to secure the loyalty not only of the masses but particularly also of all his disappointed followers, more than one of whom might well feel destined to replace him?

The whole course of human history, which is not very convincingly contradicted by the recent Russian and Polish examples, would seem to show that it is easier to establish a dictatorship than to secure the peaceful transmission of its undisputed authority from its founders to their successors.

In summing up these somewhat desultory remarks about the future of the existing dictatorships, we should, not without due hesitation, formulate our general conclusions as follows:

1. Italian fascism and German national-socialism seem today so firmly established on the double basis of their overwhelming internal force and of

[1] As Sir Charles Petrie has wittily said: ". . . . the dictator, like the mule, suffers from the weakness that he has neither pride of ancestry nor hope of posterity" (*The History of Government* [London, 1929], p. 229).

their willing or reluctant acceptance by the majority of the people, that there is no apparent reason to expect their approaching downfall.

2. Their survival would therefore seem assured as long as: (*a*) they meet with no sharp reverses as a result either of an acute and prolonged economic depression, or of a blow to their prestige from without; (*b*) they are not embroiled in a major war which would not lead to a rapid and decisive victory; (*c*) their peoples continued to stand the severe psychological and economic strain to which they are subjected but which they have so far supported with remarkable docility, fortitude, or resignation; (*d*) their leaders retain their personal life and vigor.

3. If and when any of these conditions should cease to be fulfilled, the future of the dictatorships would seem uncertain and indeed all the more jeopardized, as their internal success has been greater and the tension of their peoples more wearing and more prolonged.

4. Stalinism in Soviet Russia would seem far less secure, as it cannot point to equally successful achievements in the field of internal and especially foreign policies or boast of an equally unchallenged authority for its responsible leader.

Turning now to the consideration of the future of the surviving democracies, we are faced with an entirely different situation. In order properly to assess it, we must resort to quite different methods and apply quite different standards.

If we were to judge of dictatorships by what we hear from the countries subjected to their rule, we should be forced to the conclusion that they were led by the most infallible of leaders, supported by the unquestioned loyalty of the most enthusiastic of peoples, and therefore assured of the most glorious immortality. If, on the contrary, we were to apply the same test to the surviving democracies, we should be tempted to believe that their leaders were incapable, weak, and sometimes corrupt, that their peoples were divided into resigned followers and revolted opponents of these unfortunate leaders, and that they were doomed to imminent or at least to ultimate discredit and downfall. Such conclusions, which might be reached by a casual uninformed visitor from another planet, would, of course, be ludicrously superficial and indeed completely absurd.

It is hardly necessary to remark that a dictatorship would no more be a dictatorship if any but its eulogists were allowed publicly to discuss its policies, than a democracy would be a democracy if its critics were not free to denounce its failings. An effective articulate opposition is as characteristic of a democracy as an almighty government, intolerant of all hostile comment, is of a dictatorship.

Therefore, it is obviously not by the volume or the tone of praise or invective that we may judge of the relative popularity and accordingly of the probable future of democracies and dictatorships, but by their respective achievements. And in appraising these, we must remember that whereas democracy owes its main accomplishments to its very existence, dictatorship must justify its existence by its accomplishments.

The great virtue of democracy resides in the liberty and equality of its citizens and, therefore, in the dignity it confers upon them by reason of its fundamental principles of self-government. As long as there are people on this earth who look upon the state primarily as an instrument for the welfare of the individual and who define this welfare primarily in terms of personal freedom, then democracy, whatever its weaknesses and its inefficiencies, will be justified, if only it succeeds in maintaining itself. That this conception of a good society is shared by some but not by all our contemporaries was well shown by an exchange of views which took place during the Fourteenth Assembly of the League of Nations in 1933. On that occasion—the only one on which fully authorized representatives of National-Socialist Germany were to be heard and seen in Geneva—Reichsminister Dr. Goebbels, addressing an international

gathering of journalists, made the following characteristic statement:

Those . . . . who say that the peoples should govern themselves completely misinterpret the principle of democracy.
Nations cannot govern themselves, and they do not want to.
Their sole desire is to be governed well and they are happy
when they can have the conviction that their governments are
working to their best ability and conscience for the benefit
and welfare of the nations entrusted to them.[2]

A few days later, Mr. Ormsby-Gore, on behalf of
the British Empire, made the following reply in the
Sixth Committee:

The British Empire does not conceive of itself in terms of
racial solidarity, but in the terms of the free association of
free people . . . . bound together by what is the real guarantee
for all minorities all over the world—free self-governing institutions. We have always said: "Rather self-government than
even good government . . . . " I must allude to the challenge
of Dr. Goebbels the other day when he talked about the
obsolete character of parliamentary government. We believe that the liberties of England are based upon parliamentary government. It is an institution that has survived
in our country unbroken for six hundred and fifty years, and
neither in the name of democracy nor anything else are we
going to abandon our free parliamentary system whereby no
government shall introduce a law or a decree until it has been
discussed in the face of minorities and oppositions and been
gone through clause by clause and line by line.[3]

[2] *Völkerbund*, Journal of the German League of Nations Union,
Eng. ed. (September 29, 1933), p. 3.

[3] League of Nations, *Records of the Fourteenth Ordinary Session
of the Assembly* (Minutes of the Sixth Committee, Geneva, 1933),
pp. 35–36.

THE CRISIS OF DEMOCRACY

In this debate Dr. Goebbels and Mr. Ormsby-Gore, the present Lord Harlech, may well both have been voicing faithfully the conflicting views of their respective national constituencies. That most Englishmen and, we may add, most other Anglo-Saxons, Frenchmen, Swiss, Belgians, Dutchmen, and Scandinavians, prefer self-government, that is, democracy, even if less efficient, to dictatorship, even if more so, is, we believe, certain. But that most Germans and perhaps most Italians and other peoples prefer to be relieved of the responsibilities of governing themselves is at least quite possible. If the primary desire of the beneficiaries or victims of dictatorship is to be governed, they must certainly appreciate their present condition. Because whatever one may think of their moral, intellectual, and social plight, governed they certainly are.

For all those who share the democratic opinions so concisely expressed by the British delegate—liberty, equality, democracy, and self-government are then desirable ends in themselves. In order to remain so, even in the eyes of their most loyal devotees, they must, however, prove able to maintain themselves. Will they be able to do so?

Democracies as states are today threatened by the economic, political, and military competition of their dictatorial rivals. And democracy as a system of government is threatened by the internal policies which it has everywhere been led to adopt, but to whose technical exigencies its traditional liberal procedures are in many respects less well adapted than are those of more autocratic regimes. Let us in turn consider these two menaces and ask ourselves, in conclusion, whether and how democracy may prove able to cope with them.

The World War, as we have seen, was won by democracy. Not only were the armies of the self-governing states victorious over those of their autocratic enemies, but their ideals seemed to be very generally adopted in Europe before the final peace settlement. Since then the position has undoubtedly been reversed. Not only have the defeated powers and the new states carved out of their former empires generally reverted to autocracy in another form, but the new dictatorships have recovered the diplomatic leadership which their imperial predecessors had lost with military defeat twenty years ago. That democracy is on the defensive today in Europe cannot be denied.

The reasons for this, however, are not such as to constitute an unqualified indictment of democracy. To be sure, its diplomacy unwillingly but very unwisely promoted the rise of dictatorships in failing to secure the success of the democratic experiments it had initiated at the close of the war. But if the dictatorships are calling the

tune in foreign policy today, it is essentially because of the admittedly and professedly greater
love of peace which animates their democratic
rivals. To blame the latter for the concessions they
have made and are making to the former, in the
hope of thus avoiding a renewal of the horrors of
the World War, may be to reproach them with inferior foresight and intelligence. But it is at the
same time to pay a tribute to their superior
morality.

A law-abiding citizen who, for fear of the general
consequences, turns over his purse to a threatening gangster in a crowded restaurant instead of
shooting him first, is no hero. But of the gangster
and his victim, the blackguard is certainly not the
latter.

History may well prove that, having failed to
avoid the rise of aggressive dictatorships by generous diplomacy, democracy would have been well
advised to disarm them by force before they became too formidable. But it will no more thereby
vindicate dictatorship or condemn democracy than
it today proclaims the superior humanity and the
higher civilization of Macedonia over the Athenian
city-state of the fourth century B.C. If, in spite of
the clearly provocative policies of the dictatorships, peace is maintained in Europe, it will re-
dound to the glory of democracy, to whose forbearance it will manifestly be due. But even if it

should come to the worst, that forbearance may still find its justification in the evolution of the future.

In 1918 the democratic Allies would probably not have been victorious had it not become the general conviction first of their own peoples, then of the neutrals, and finally even among many of their enemies, that they were the pacific victims of the aggressive ambitions of their imperial opponents. If the question of the war guilt played such a part in the issue of the World War, when it was much more debatable, might it not again prove a decisive factor, now that it would be so much less so than twenty-four years ago?

Narrowly nationalistic and dangerously threatening as it has been in its inspirations, the diplomacy of the dictators has often since the war been efficient in its intimidating methods and, therefore, effective. And, on the other hand, deliberately pacific as has in general been that of the democracies in its inspirations, it has often been shortsighted, feeble, and vacillating in its conciliatory methods and, therefore, ineffective. If international politics were a mere game, the scores of the dictatorial teams would undoubtedly stand higher today than those of their democratic rivals. But in this field, as in many others, the display of better sportsmanship may in the long run count for more than the winning of points by questionable methods. Humiliating and indeed disquieting as is the present diplomatic situation for the democratic states, it is a most honorable inferiority to which they are condemned, in face of the dictatorships, by their greater love of peace.

If war were to break out, it would be a catastrophe for all. But it seems difficult to believe that it would not in the end again be won by democracy and that it would not again lead to the downfall of autocracy. Not only are the natural resources of the self-governing states far greater, but the courage and endurance of their peoples, struggling for their liberty, could hardly in the long run fail to prove superior to those of their opponents, led to slaughter by their dictatorial masters. Furthermore, the technical advantages enjoyed by the latter in the preparations for war in time of peace would soon be neutralized, because under the stress of war and for its duration the democracies would again be led to adopt similarly effective dictatorial methods. In fact, the dictatorships would forfeit the relative benefit of their bellicose methods at the very moment when these methods had led to the outbreak of general hostilities and, therefore, to their universal adoption. These methods we do not hesitate to define as bellicose, because they are clearly inspired by the greater fear of war, or rather by the more ardent love of peace, which the Rome-Berlin axis rightly ascribes to its Franco-British rivals. It is surely a case of the bellicism of the former speculating on the pacifism of the latter.

The apparent and provisional superiority enjoyed by the dictators at this dangerous game is not what concerns us most in considering the future of democracy. It is rather the dangers which threaten it from within.

Modern democracy, as we have seen, owes its origin to a revolt against the restrictions on the liberty of the individual and against the social and political inequalities which absolutism in its various national forms had imposed upon its subjects. The democratic program, therefore, called for the damming-back of the state and for the emancipation of the citizen from the pressure to which it had long subjected him. Self-government was looked upon as the best and fairest means for attaining these ends.

Now, when democracy had been set up, government by the people and of the people immediately led to government for the people. And the people were not long content with the freedom from oppression and discrimination they had achieved. They soon realized that, whereas the political and economic liberty they had striven for and secured had relieved them of one set of grievances, it had not as appreciably improved their material lot, as they had been led to hope and to expect. Indeed they found that what they had gained in nominal freedom—to pursue as they pleased the economic activities of their choice unhampered by any social control—they had lost in security. They discovered also that political privileges based on inequalities of birth were not the only privileges or the most irritating inequalities. Whereas their former rulers had been their traditional masters, but often also their traditional protectors, they had, by freeing themselves of their rulers, deprived themselves of their recent protectors. And the new masters, who had arisen as a natural consequence of freely competitive conditions, were the less inclined to assume any responsibility of protection, as they owed their mastery not to their inherited position of social superiority but only to their own individual efforts.

Under these conditions the people naturally turned to the state, over which they had secured control. They demanded that it should curb the activities of their new industrial masters when these activities jeopardized their own welfare, that it should take over the duties of their former traditional rulers and protect them against the risks inherent in economic freedom, and that it should use its financial authority to improve their intellectual and social lot and to limit and correct the inequalities of income to which natural ability and inherited wealth were more and more giving rise under the newly established conditions of free competition.

Whence, labor legislation forbidding the employment of children and limiting the hours and fixing the conditions of work for adults, and then protecting them against the consequences of accident, illness, old age, and unemployment. Whence also the promotion of universal, compulsory, and gratuitous education by the establishment and development of state-financed schools. Whence also the gradually extended control of the state over all industrial, commercial, and banking enterprises tending toward the transference of the means of production from private to public ownership. Whence also the gradual turning-over of a larger and larger part of the national income to the state, by means of increasingly graduated taxation of private incomes, private savings, and private inheritance. Whence, finally, a huge growth of public indebtedness and the gradual emergence of an increasingly elaborate, technically complicated, and financially burdensome piece of social machinery, over which democracy itself, which had willed its creation and its development, could no longer exercise effective control.

That process, which I have studied in some detail in Switzerland,[4] has been going on in all demo-

[4] *L'Individu et l'Etat*, etc.

cratic countries. Indeed, similar technical conditions have given rise to similar developments in all capitalistic countries. But whereas this process, which has enormously enhanced and complicated the task of all governments, has tended to strengthen rather than weaken the power of autocracy, it has everywhere challenged the possibilities of democratic rule. The more complex a problem of administration, the greater the need for authority on top and of discipline below. And the greater, consequently, the relative advantages of autocracy and the more baffling the difficulties confronting democracy.

This we look upon as the supreme political problem of the age and the most dangerous threat for the future of popular government. It is coming more and more to be considered as such by all impartial and thoughtful students, as Mr. Lippmann's recent *Good Society*, for instance, indicates.[5] It is coming to be appreciated that a much closer and more intimate connection than was long suspected exists between political and economic liberty. Both these ideals were proclaimed and realized by modern democracy at its birth. But, little by little, under the pressure of compelling circumstances and, as we have seen, as the natural corollary of democratic logic, the exercise of politi-

[5] Walter Lippmann, *An Inquiry into the Principles of the Good Society* (Boston, 1937).

cal liberty led to the suppression of economic liberty. And today the most ardent advocates of democratic progress, as the Socialists like to consider themselves, were and are most insistent in their demands that freedom should be curtailed in favor of equality and that the state should become, not only the chief arbiter of all individual destinies, but also the great organizer of the national life and the principal distributor of the national income.

The more successful they are in their efforts, the more difficult becomes the problem of political democracy. Should they ever fully succeed in any of our advanced states, as they have nearly done in Soviet Russia, the problem would be rendered entirely insoluble here, as it has been there. Only a dictatorship, and not even a dictatorship of the proletariat such as Karl Marx had foreseen, could hope to administer his classless state. In such a state, all individuals would be reduced to the functions of infinitesimal parts of an infinitely large and complex machine. To run such a machine effectively would take the undivided attention and the undisputed will of one chief engineer. The almost superhuman task of the latter would obviously become hopeless, had he, before reaching his decisions, to consult all the countless organs under his orders, or even a small body representing some of them.

THE CRISIS OF DEMOCRACY

The parts of an engine driven by one central motor must be inanimate and inarticulate if it is to run smoothly or even to work at all, and if destruction and chaos are to be avoided. Likewise democracy is not conceivable if all activities are to spring from, to be controlled by, or to be concentrated in, one almighty and all embracing state. A rowing crew can govern itself if it is wise enough to intrust to its self-chosen captain certain directing and co-ordinating functions. A locomotive cannot.

If our previous analysis is correct, the difficulties arising from the conflict between political liberty and economic equality are inherent in democracy under the technical conditions of modern civilization. They would have to be faced even if mankind was not divided into politically sovereign but economically interdependent states. The existence of a multiplicity of such states, however, and especially the intense rivalry and hostility which today oppose them one to another, still further enhance the difficulties of modern democracy.

During the World War, as we have seen, all the democracies temporarily resigned their rights and liberties into the hands of their leaders. International war necessarily calls for prompt, swift, and ruthless action by the state and complete subordination of the individual. It therefore, in

THE FUTURE OF DEMOCRACY

democratic states, inevitably leads to a suspension
of democracy. Democracy is a child of peace and
cannot live apart from its mother.[6]

But have we peace in the world today?

Even if all national armies are not fully mobi-
lized, it can be said that all states not actually
engaged in war are living under the threat of war
and are shaping not only their military but also
their economic policies with a view to war. It
would lead us too far afield if we were here to recall the countless consequences which spring from
this undoubted fact. It is enough for our present
purposes to point to the desire for national self-
sufficiency which dominates all commercial policies. This desire directly leads to high and constantly changing tariffs, to quotas and prohibi-
tions, and indirectly to all the other means of
regulating international trade, such as clearing
arrangements, export subsidies, and managed and
fluctuating currencies.[7]

Now all the devices to which states resort in
order to control their natural resources and to
combat industrial unemployment call for increased
governmental intervention and, therefore, for reduced individual freedom. Less, to be sure, than

[6] Cf. Bourquin, "The Crisis of Democracy," in *The World Crisis*,
p. 69: "The climate of democracy is peace and prosperity."

[7] Cf. W. E. Rappard, *Post-war Efforts for Freer Trade* ("Geneva
Studies" [March, 1938]).

in times of open war, but far more than in times of assured peace, democracy is obliged today to submit to an eclipse of its rights and liberties. Decisions such as those relating to national defense, tariff negotiations, and monetary devaluations, can obviously not be submitted to a popular referendum. As a rule, they cannot even be freely debated in a democratic parliament. Sometimes they cannot even be openly discussed in a responsible ministry. By their very nature, they must often be taken without any publicity by irresponsible officials, over whose action governments have little, parliaments less, and the people no control whatever.

The crisis of democracy, owing to the general and more permanent causes we have analyzed above, is therefore intensified by these special circumstances, which we may look upon as temporary, but which are dangerously compelling today.

The future of democracy, therefore, depends in the first instance on the maintenance of peace and on the organization of international relations such as will again allow national governments to strive primarily for the prosperity of their people and no longer oblige them to subordinate it to the security of their states. But even if and when this be achieved, democracy will still have to face its major problem: that of so organizing the state as to make it both efficient and truly responsive to the will of the people, while protecting and not endangering the individual liberty of its citizens.

That problem is obviously not susceptible of any simple and easy solution. We do not, however, as do the dictatorial cynics and the democratic pessimists, hold it to be insoluble. It cannot be our task at the close of these brief and still all too long chapters on the crisis of democracy to consider any solutions in detail. Suffice it to say that we should look for such solutions in two directions.

On the one hand, our efforts would tend to relieve the state of many of the burdens under which it is staggering today and under which it cannot remain either responsive to the will of the people or respectful of their primary liberties. As we see it, the defense of democracy demands a return to greater economic freedom, without which no state, however organized, can give its citizens more than the illusion of governing themselves. If the political will of the people is again to become supreme, it must be content to assert itself over a more limited domain. It is, therefore, not only because we believe private enterprise to be more creative, more progressive, more efficient, and consequently productive of greater general prosperity than that of the state, that we venture to advocate a limitation of the latter. It is also because we believe that no state that has been allowed to become totalitarian in its activities can fail to become totalitarian in its claims on the subservience of its subjects. Our plea for more private liberty is, therefore, political no less than economic.

We need hardly add that ours is not, however, a plea for a return to complete laissez faire. The historical conditions which jusified this demand were those of an age when the state interfered with economic life mainly to protect individual privilege and to inhibit individual initiative. Those conditions have happily been washed away by the wave of political and economic liberty which swept over the democratic countries of Europe a century ago.

In their place, however, new conditions of privilege and of monopoly have sprung up, both in the sphere of capital and in that of labor, again more or less indirectly fostered rather than effectively combated by the state. These conditions it is the obvious duty of democracy not to tolerate by its inaction, still less to favor by its interventions, but, on the contrary, to prevent and to suppress by its vigilance.

As the technical economic and social circumstances of today are no longer comparable to those prevailing a century ago, so the polity of the democratic state cannot be the same. The creation of large-scale enterprise, the accumulation and concentration of capital, and the increase of population, have fundamentally altered and inevitably enlarged the tasks of government. But its purpose should remain the same, and that purpose, we hold, should still be to protect and not to inhibit individual freedom.

As a policeman intrusted with the duty of regulating the traffic on a busy street corner in a crowded metropolis must display more authority and greater activity than a country constable in a rural hamlet, so government today cannot be content with the role played by its predecessors in the quieter circumstances of a century ago. Again the measure and the kind of individual liberty enjoyed by the New Yorker and the Chicagoan cannot be the same as that to which his social isolation entitles the mountaineer in a Swiss Alpine village as a compensation for all the amenities of civilization, including the contacts with gangsterism, of which he is deprived. So no industrial community of our day can claim the same measure and the same kind of freedom from state control and state supervision as that enjoyed by our forefathers at the beginning of the nineteenth century.

But if we wish to remain our own masters, as they successfully sought to become, we must insist that the state remain, as they wished that the state become, a servant of the people and not their tyrant. Nor should we forget that the worst tyrants are not infrequently those to whose whims and caprices we are subjected less by reason of their overbearance than by that of our self-indulgence. A pampered bachelor, tormented and exploited by an originally dutiful cook whose services have become indispensable to his voluptuous well-being, is neither as free nor as prosperous as his sturdier neighbor who prepares his own food. It would often seem as if modern democracies, in their demands upon the state as well as in their submission to its exactions, more closely resembled the pampered bachelor than his sturdier neighbor.

However, it is clear that the state, even if relieved of many of its present functions, must, under the conditions of industrial civilization, remain a most impressive institution, charged with heavy and multifarious duties. As an instrument for the expression and for the execution of the will of the people, it will, therefore, always remain most cumbersome and unwieldy. How to organize it so that it may best obey and serve but not crush its popular master will, therefore, always be the main problem of democracy.

Between the citizen who commands and the civil servant who is finally to carry out his orders, there must inevitably be several intermediaries. Of these, the most important and the least avoidable are the political party which crystallizes the citizen's wishes into a collective program, the parliament which translates this program into legislative principles, and the executive which implements these principles by means of ordinances, decrees, and instructions to its officials.

In the course of this procedure it may well happen that the original wishes of the citizen are misunderstood, misinterpreted, or even wilfully perverted by his representatives. It may of course also happen that they are successfully opposed by other more strongly supported wishes. The most perfect democracy is that in which the wishes of the majority are the most faithfully and the most promptly executed by the civil servants. The greater the discrepancies and the longer the delays, the further removed from its ideal prototype is the democratic state in question.

As one may observe that the legislature is more often responsible for these discrepancies and delays than the other organs, it is usually here that reform may most usefully set in. To abolish the legislature and to transfer all its functions to the executive may be dangerous for liberty. But if democratic government is to be made more efficient, more honest, and more obedient to the will of the people, it is certainly in the concentration of power in the hands of those immediately responsible for its exercise that the future lies.

The more numerous and the more difficult the tasks confided to democracy and the keener the competition of dictatorships, the greater must be the authority and the wider the prerogatives of those chosen by the people to lead them. The real safeguards of public liberty must be sought not in parliamentary interference but in the jealously protected freedom of the opposition and in the absolute independence of the judiciary. The stronger the government, the wider and the more secure must be the freedom of speech, of association, and of the press, lest the effort to equip democracy for its struggle against dictatorship end in the subversion of democracy itself into dictatorship.

In speculating about the future of popular government as in considering its past, one cannot fail to realize that, important as may be questions of constitutional organization, they are infinitely less so than the character, temper, and education of the peoples themselves. Political liberty and equality are not free gifts with which an indifferent people may be once for all endowed by a generous legislator. They are stern principles which must be imposed by a strong people on a willing legislator, who must be constantly reminded of their sanctity and held to account for their violation by a vigilant public opinion.

The future of democracy, therefore, lies primarily with the democratic peoples themselves.

THE FUTURE OF DEMOCRACY

The historian, the economist, and the student of political science can enlighten and warn. That, to the best of our modest ability, we have sought to do in these pages. But he can no more save democracy from itself and from its foes than a writer on military topics can insure the discipline of an army and win its battles.

Our studies have not led us to despair of modern democracy, but rather to question the solidity and the longevity of modern dictatorship. But they have also led us to realize that the future of democracy depends upon the character of the democratic peoples and upon the wisdom and courage of their leaders, still more than does the future of dictatorship on the ability of dictators.

May our free peoples remain worthy of the high destiny to which their forefathers have dedicated them by their efforts and by their sacrifices! And may they, by the example of their virtues and of their achievements, win over to their generous ideals of life and of society their neighbors who are today still unwilling or unable to govern themselves! Those are my hopes, not only for all the peoples, free and unfree alike, but for the future of peace in our time and of civilization itself. Let this, my final word, be a message of hope addressed by a citizen of the oldest, to his friends of the greatest democracy in the world.

BIBLIOGRAPHY

ACTON, LORD. *Lectures on Modern History*. London, 1926.

ADLER, MAX. *Démocratie politique et démocratie sociale*. Brussels, 1930.

AMERICAN ACADEMY OF POLITICAL AND SOCIAL SCIENCE. *The Crisis of Democracy*. Philadelphia, 1933.

———. *Socialism, Fascism and Democracy*. Philadelphia, 1935.

AMREIN, A. *Volk ohne Führung*. Zurich, 1937.

ANDRASSY, COUNT J. *Diplomacy and the War*. London, 1921.

ARCHAMBAULT, P. *Réalisme démocratique*. Paris, 1930.

ARMSTRONG, H. F. *We or They: Two Worlds in Conflict*. New York, 1937.

ASQUITH, C., and SPENDER, J. A. *Life of Herbert Henry Asquith*. 2 vols. London, 1932.

ASQUITH, H. H. *Memories and Reflections*. 2 vols. London, 1928.

———. *Speeches by the Earl of Oxford and Asquith*. New York, 1927.

ASSOCIATION JURID. INTERNAT. *Régression des principes de liberté dans les réformes constitutionnelles de certains états démocratiques*. Paris, 1938.

AULARD, A. *Histoire politique de la Révolution française*. Paris, 1905.

BABBITT, IRVING. *Democracy and Leadership*. Boston, 1929.

BARTHÉLEMY, JOSEPH. *La Conduite de la politique extérieure dans les démocraties*. Paris, 1930.

———. *Le Problème de la compétence dans la démocratie*. Paris, 1918.

———. *Valeur de la liberté et adaptation de la république*. Paris, 1935.

BATTAGLIA, O. F. DE (ed.). *Prozess der Diktatur*. Vienna, 1930.

BIBLIOGRAPHY

BAUER, O. *Zwischen zwei Weltkriegen? Die Krise der Welt-wirtschaft, der Demokratie und des Sozialismus.* Bratislava, 1936.

BENOIST, CHARLES. *Les Maladies de la démocratie.* Paris, 1929.

BERDYAEV, NICOLAS. *The Origin of Russian Communism.* Trans. from the Russian. London, 1937.

BONN, M. J. *The Crisis of European Democracy.* (German trans., Munich.) New Haven, 1925.

BORGEAUD, CHARLES. *The Rise of Modern Democracy in Old and New England.* London, 1894.

———. *Pages d'histoire nationale.* Geneva, 1934.

BOUGLÉ, C. *La Démocratie devant la science.* Paris, 1923.

BOURGIN, H. *Quand tout le monde est roi, la crise de la démo-cratie.* Paris, 1929.

BOURQUIN, MAURICE. "The Crisis of Democracy," in *The World Crisis,* by the PROFESSORS OF THE GRADUATE IN-STITUTE OF INTERNATIONAL STUDIES. London, 1938.

BRAILSFORD, H. N. *Property or Peace.* London, 1934.

BROOKING, R. S. *Economic Democracy.* New York, 1929.

BRYCE, JAMES. *Modern Democracies.* 2 vols. 3d ed. London, 1923.

BURNS, C. DELISLE. *Democracy: Its Defects and Advantages.* London, 1929.

CAMBO, F. *Les Dictatures.* Paris, 1930.

Cambridge Modern History, Vol. III. Cambridge, 1907.

CHARDON, G. H. *L'Organisation d'une démocratie.* Paris, 1921.

CLEVELAND, F. A. *Democracy in Reconstruction.* Boston, 1919.

COXE, WILLIAM. *Travels in Switzerland.* 3 vols. 4th ed. London, 1801.

DEHERME, G. *L'immense question de l'ordre.* Paris, 1930.

DELBRÜCK, H. *Government and the Will of the People.* New York, 1923.

FINER, H. *Mussolini's Italy.* London, 1935.

FLEINER, F. *Schweizerisches Bundesstaatsrecht.* Tübingen, 1923.

THE CRISIS OF DEMOCRACY

FLOTTES, P. *La Démocratie entre deux abîmes.* Paris, 1929.

FOLLETT, M. P. *The New State.* New York, 1920.

GASCOIN, E. *Réforme de l'Etat.* Paris, 1932.

GIRAUD, E. *La Crise de la démocratie et le renforcement du pouvoir exécutif.* Paris, 1938.

GISBORNE, F. A. W. *Democracy on Trial.* London, 1928.

GRAHAM, M. W. *New Governments of Central Europe.* London, 1924.

———. *New Governments of Eastern Europe.* London, 1928.

GREY, VISCOUNT. *Twenty-five Years.* 2 vols. London, 1926.

GUY-GRAND, C. *L'Avenir de la démocratie.* Paris, 1928.

HADLEY, A. T. *Economic Problems of Democracy.* Cambridge, Mass., 1923.

———. *The Moral Basis of Democracy.* New Haven, 1919.

———. *The Relations between Freedom and Responsibility in the Evolution of Democratic Government.* New Haven, 1921.

HATTERSLEY, A. F. *A Short History of Democracy.* Cambridge, 1930.

HEIDEN, KONRAD. *Hitler: A Biography.* London, 1936.

HERMENS, F. A. *Demokratie und Kapitalismus.* Munich, 1931.

HEUSS, THEODOR. *Hitlers Weg.* Berlin, 1932.

HITLER, ADOLF. *Mein Kampf.* 42d ed. Munich, 1933.

HOBSON, J. A. *Democracy and a Changing Civilization.* London, 1934.

HOLCOMBE, A. N. *The Foundations of the Modern Commonwealth.* New York, 1923.

HOOVER, H. C. *The Challenge to Liberty.* New York, 1934.

HUBERT, R. *Le Principe d'autorité dans l'organisation démocratique.* Paris, 1926.

HUME, DAVID. *Essays Literary, Moral and Political.* 3d ed. Edinburgh, 1748.

KELSEN, HANS. *Vom Wesen und Wert der Demokratie.* Tübingen, 1929.

KERENSKY, A. F. *The Catastrophe.* New York, 1927.

KRAUS, H. *The Crisis of German Democracy.* Princeton, 1932.

BIBLIOGRAPHY

LASKI, H. J. *Authority in the Modern State*. New Haven, 1919.
———. *The Foundations of Sovereignty*. London, 1921.
———. *Democracy in Crisis*. London, 1933.
LAUN, R. *La Démocratie*. Paris, 1933.
LEAGUE OF NATIONS. *Records of the Fourteenth Ordinary Session of the Assembly: Minutes of the Sixth Committee*. Geneva, 1933.
LECKY, W. E. H. *Democracy and Liberty*. 2 vols. London, 1896.
LEIBHOLZ, G. *Die Auflösung der liberalen Demokratie*. Munich, 1933.
LEINERT, M. *Volksstaat oder Diktatur?* Gotha, 1930.
LENIN, V. I. *Selected Works*, Vol. VI. London, 1936.
LETTERLÉ, H. *Fascisme, communisme ou démocratie*. Paris, 1929.
LINDSAY, A. D. *The Essentials of Democracy*. Oxford, 1929.
LIPPMANN, WALTER. *An Inquiry into the Principles of the Good Society*. Boston, 1937.
LLOYD GEORGE, DAVID. *War Memoirs*. 6 vols. London, 1933–36.
LOCKE, JOHN. *Two Treatises of Government*. London, 1698.
LOWELL, A. LAWRENCE. *Public Opinion and Popular Government*. New York, 1913.
MACAULAY, T. B. *The History of England from the Accession of James the Second*, Vol. I. Fireside ed. Boston and New York, 1910.
———. *Speeches and Legal Studies*. Fireside ed. Boston and New York, 1910.
MACKINDER, H. J. *Democratic Ideals and Reality*. London, 1919.
McKINLEY, S. B. *Democracy and Military Power*. New York, 1934.
MADARIAGA, S. DE. *Anarchie ou hiérarchie: la crise de la démocratie*. Paris, 1936.
MAINE, SIR HENRY SUMNER. *Popular Government*. London, 1885.

MARRIOTT, J. A. R. *The Mechanism of the Modern State.* 2 vols. Oxford, 1927.

———. *Dictatorship and Democracy.* Oxford, 1935.

MASARYK, T. G. *Les Problèmes de la démocratie.* Paris, 1924.

MASSABUAU, J. *L'Etat contre la nation.* Paris, 1922.

MATHEWS, SHAILER. *The Validity of American Ideals.* Cincinnati, 1922.

MAURRAS, C. M. P. *Les Princes des nuées.* Paris, 1928.

MICHELS, R. *Zur Soziologie des Parteiwesens in der modernen Demokratie.* 2d ed. Leipzig, 1925.

MILHAUD, E. *La Société des Nations.* Paris, 1917.

MILIUKOV, PAUL. *Russlands Zusammenbruch.* 2 vols. Berlin, 1925.

MIRKINE-GUETZEVITCH, B. *Les Constitutions de l'Europe nouvelle.* 2d ed. Paris, 1930.

MITWALLY, A. H. *La Démocratie et la représentation des intérêts en France.* Paris, 1931.

MUSSOLINI, BENITO. *Edition définitive des œuvres et discours.* French trans. 10 vols. Paris.

———. *My Autobiography.* New York, 1928.

———. *Le Fascisme.* Paris, 1933.

NEWBOLD, W. *Democracy, Debts and Disarmament.* London, 1934.

NITTI, F. S. *Bolshevism, Fascism and Democracy.* London, 1927.

———. *La Démocratie.* 2 vols. Paris, 1933.

PENMAN, J. S. *The Irresistible Movement of Democracy.* London, 1923.

PERCY, LORD EUSTACE. *Democracy on Trial.* London, 1931.

PETRIE, SIR CHARLES. *The History of Government.* London, 1929.

PINK, M. A. *A Realist Looks at Democracy.* London, 1930.

POINCARÉ, RAYMOND. *Au Service de la France,* Vol. IV: Paris, 1927; Vol. V: Paris, 1928.

RAPPARD, W. E. *Uniting Europe: The Trend of International Cooperation since the War.* New Haven, 1930.

———. *L'Individu et l'Etat dans l'évolution constitutionnelle de la Suisse.* Zurich, 1936.

BIBLIOGRAPHY

————. *Post-war Efforts for Freer Trade.* ("Geneva Studies.") Geneva, 1938.

————. *Post-war Efforts for Freer Trade.* ("Geneva Studies.") March, 1938.

————. *The Government of Switzerland.* New York, 1936.

Rapport du Conseil fédéral à l'Assemblée fédérale sur l'initiative tendant à restreindre l'emploi de la clause d'urgence du 10 mai 1938.

REALE, EGIDIO. *L'Italie.* Paris, 1934.

RIGNANO, E. *Democrazia e fascismo.* Milan, 1924.

RIPERT, G. *Le Régime démocratique et le droit civil.* Paris, 1936.

ROBERTS, R. *The Unfinished Program of Democracy.* New York, 1920.

ROSENBERG, ARTHUR. *A History of the German Republic.* Trans. from the German. London, 1936.

ROUSSEAU, J. J. *Le Contrat Social.* 1762.

SCHUMAN, F. L. *Hitler and the Nazi Dictatorship.* London, 1936.

SEMBAT, MARCEL. *Faites un roi, sinon faites la paix.* Paris, 1913.

SERVENTI, G. N. *Ascesa della democrazia europea e prime reazioni storiche.* Rome, 1925.

SPENDER, J. A., and ASQUITH, C. *Life of Herbert Henry Asquith.* 2 vols. London, 1932.

SPENGLER, OSWALD. *Der Untergang des Abendlandes.* 2 vols. Munich, 1927.

SPRING RICE, SIR CECIL. *The Letters and Friendships of Sir Cecil Spring Rice.* Ed. STEPHEN GWYNN. 2 vols. London, 1929.

STALIN, JOSEPH. *Leninism.* Trans. from the Russian. 2 vols. London, 1928-33.

STAMPFER, FRIEDRICH. *Die vierzehn Jahre der ersten Deutschen Republik.* Karlsbad, 1936.

STEED, WICKHAM, and OTHERS. *Les Démocraties modernes.* Paris, 1921.

THE CRISIS OF DEMOCRACY

STIMSON, H. L. *Democracy and Nationalism in Europe.* Princeton, 1934.

STURZO, DON LUIGI. *Italy and Fascismo.* London, 1926.

SUTTON, C. *Farewell to Rousseau: A Critique of Liberal Democracy.* London, 1936.

TEMPERLEY, H. W. V. (ed.). *A History of the Peace Conference of Paris,* Vol. I. London, 1920.

TINGSTEN, H. *Les pleins pouvoirs.* Trans. from the Swedish. Paris, 1934.

TRENTIN, SILVIO. *Antidémocratie.* Paris, 1930.

TROTSKY, LEON. *The History of the Russian Revolution.* Trans. from the Russian. 3 vols. London, 1932–34.

VILLARI, LUIGI. *Italy.* London, 1929.

Völkerbund (journal of the German League of Nations Union). September 29, 1933.

WELLS, H. G. *After Democracy.* London, 1932.

WEYL, W. E. *The New Democracy.* New York, 1919.

WILSON, W. *President Wilson's State Papers and Addresses.* New York, 1918.

WOOLF, L., and OTHERS. *The Modern State.* London, 1933.

ZIMMERN, SIR ALFRED. *The Greek Commonwealth.* Oxford, 1915.

———. *The Prospects of Democracy.* London, 1929.

ZURCHER, A. J. *The Experiment with Democracy in Central Europe.* New York, 1933.

INDEX

INDEX

Acton, Lord, 44–45 (quoted)

American Academy of Political and Social Science, 184

Amrein, A., 185, 225

Andorra, 102

Andrassy, Count J., 112

Anticommunistic legislation, 222 ff.

Anti-Semitism. *See* Jews

Appenzell, 62

Archambault, P., 184, 200

Armstrong, H. F., 185

Asquith, C., 78

Asquith, H. H. (Earl of Oxford and Asquith), 74–75, 77–78 (quoted), 78, 81–82 (quoted), 87 ff. (quoted), 89 f.

Assembly, National Constituent, 15, 53

Athens, 32 f., 63, 256

Aulard, A., 53, 59

Austria, 103, 107, 112 ff., 137, 143, 230, 246

Austria-Hungary, 85, 103, 161

Avanti, 139, 159

Babbitt, Irving, 184

Baltic States, 230

Barthélemy, Joseph, 183 f., 189 f. (quoted), 193, 200

Bastille, 56

Battisti, Cesare, 139

Bauer, O., 185

Belgium, 67, 83 ff., 117, 232

Benes, President, 109

Benoist, Charles, 184

Berdyaev, N., 129 (quoted)

Berlin, 180, 236

Berne, 64

Bill of Rights, 44, 53

Bonn, M. J., 184

Borgeaud, Charles, 43

Bourgeoisie, 1, 56, 58, 125, 127, 169

Bourgin, H., 184

Bourquin, M., 19, 83, 265

Brailsford, H. N., 184

Brest-Litovsk, 161

Briand, A., 74, 91 (quoted), 164

Bryce, Viscount, 3–4 (quoted), 5 f., 30 (quoted), 61 (quoted), 67, 202, 203

Bulgaria, 102, 117

Burns, C. Delisle, 184, 203

Callender, C. N., 184

Calvin, John, 41

Calvinism, 43

Censorship, 82

Chamber of Deputies, Italian, 146, 151 f.

Chardon, G. H., 183

Charles, Emperor of Austria, 112

〖 283 〗

THE CRISIS OF DEMOCRACY

INDEX

INDEX